D1384230

THE UNITED STATES
AND THE FUTURE OF THAILAND

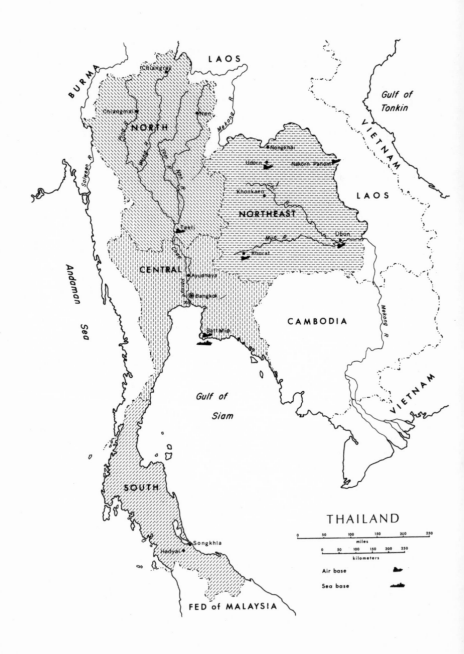

BURMA

LAOS

{Chiengrai

Chiangmai

NORTH

Nan

Salween R.

Ping R.

Wang R.

Yom R.

Nan R.

Mekong R.

Nongkhai

Udorn

Nakorn Panom

Khonkaen

NORTHEAST

LAOS

Takli

Mun R.

Ubon

CENTRAL

Khurat

Menam Chao Praya R.

Ayudhaya

Bangkok

Sattahip

CAMBODIA

Mekong R.

VIETNAM

Gulf of
Tonkin

Andaman
Sea

Gulf of
Siam

VIETNAM

SOUTH

THAILAND

Songkhla

Hadyai

0   50   100   150   200   250
miles

0   50   100   150   200   250
kilometers

Air base

Sea base

FED of MALAYSIA

The United States
and the Future of Thailand

David A. Wilson

PRAEGER PUBLISHERS

New York · Washington · London

PRAEGER PUBLISHERS
111 Fourth Avenue, New York, N.Y. 10003, U.S.A.
5, Cromwell Place, London S.W.7, England

Published in the United States of America in 1970
by Praeger Publishers, Inc.

Library of Congress Catalog Card Number: 70–95697

Printed in the United States of America

To my friends at Kyodai

I want to acknowledge the help of the participants in the seminar at the Center for Southeast Asian Studies, Kyoto University, held in the spring of 1968, as well as that of Albert Williams, Judith Bernstein, Cynthia Horan, and Kathryn Gardner, without suggesting that any of them bears any responsibility for this book or shares my views.

Contents

Tables and Chart

The frontispiece of this volume is a map of Thailand.

THE UNITED STATES
AND THE FUTURE OF THAILAND

Introduction

America is facing a crisis in foreign affairs, a crisis precipitated by war in Southeast Asia. The Vietnam war is too costly in men and material and has continued too long. The quest for a settlement in Vietnam is a priority for the President and people of the United States, but they seek a satisfactory settlement, one which holds promise of some degree of peace in Vietnam and Southeast Asia in the future. Such a settlement has proved elusive.

What is Southeast Asia, and why has it become so troublesome to the United States? How did the United States get involved in Southeast Asia? Is the cost of this involvement worth the benefits to be gained from it? What is the future of this turbulent region? The American people, pondering the agony of Vietnam, urgently need answers to these questions. But there are no clear and simple answers, particularly to those questions that demand assessments of value to the United States.

There are no clear and simple answers to these questions, because uncertainty is a fundamental characteristic of the Southeast Asian region. The states of Southeast Asia have emerged within a course of events that is little understood, exceedingly dynamic, and inherently unpredictable. During the past 150 years, the increasing power of European states—principally Great Britain, France, and The Netherlands—worked toward the creation of a new political map of Southeast Asia. The European empires established the rudiments of new political communities that seemed to serve as the basis for autonomous states. But these empires were destroyed before the new communities were well formed, although after the foundations of old communities had been dissolved. Since it is the cohesion of communities as they relate to each other that serves to give regularity to human events, the incomplete transformation of communities in Southeast Asia is essentially ambiguous.

We cannot know the future, regardless of our hopes or our revulsion from its unknown threats. But it is in the character of our age, in which the fragile web of civilization links the peoples of the world, that Americans seek to control this dark future and that we are doomed to grapple with its ambiguities. The United States is no longer a mere model, a *Novus Ordo Seclorum*. The effects of American productivity, our currency, our weaponry, and our consumption are experienced everywhere, and, for that reason, we are impelled to influence people and events. Simultaneously, we find ourselves engaged in an effort to realize our vision of human life, however vague and imperfect that vision may be. We carry on this struggle in this country and abroad by policy and politics, by persuasion and force, by leadership and attraction, and by whatever moral means we can muster. We do so in order to create and preserve the forms of life that we value. To so struggle is to serve our interests.

This struggle is, for the most part, among men because, to a great extent, the war with nature has been won. We possess the technical means to maintain humane, even comfortable, life for people, but we find ourselves engaged in a conflict of visions as to the meaning of the good life and the ordering of men and resources that the realization of the good life would require. From this clash, from this dialectic of visions, the future will be realized.

Paradoxically, in Southeast Asia, with its weakness and poverty, with its indeterminate future, the most vivid possibilities may be imagined. This possibility of possibilities draws the attention of the powers of the world—the United States, the Soviet Union, the European nations, Japan, and China —who seek to encourage or impose their visions of the future. At the same time, the leaders of Southeast Asian states ponder their potentialities and manipulate their resources, however meager, toward their own envisioned future.

In this region of agitation, be it a maelstrom or a backwater eddy, amazing things are sure to happen. The powers of the world have said that much is at stake. It appears that the stake is not only the products of forest and fields, mines and mills but also the possibility of humane life for not just some but all men.

The shifting and fragile relationships of peoples have tended to attract intervention in Southeast Asia, notably from the United States and the Soviet Union, but also from Asian countries, whether they are powerful or not. Most simply, this course of events can be understood as involving three kinds of forces—the Communist, the Western, and the indigenous. The strategies of these forces, if so portentous a word as strategies is appropriate, have deeply influenced each other.

Within this fluid scene, "containing Communism" has been the implementing doctrine from which policies and programs of the West, particularly the United States, have been derived. "Excluding American imperialism and neo-colonialism" has served as a coordinate doctrine for the Communist, particularly Chinese, side. More recently the pattern of conflicts has been complicated by divergence within both the Communist and Western sides. The Soviet Union seeks to enlarge its influence apart from, and in competition with, China. France also has sought to re-establish a position outside the framework of American policy. Both work upon the wide range of doctrines of Southeast Asian leaders, who have all sought to enhance the autonomy of their states.

Communism in both China and Vietnam has served as a foundation for political cohesion and, thus, as a source of power. Moreover, in these states, the political leaders of state and party have consistently sought to reduce or eliminate the influence of the United States. The vision of future life and politics projected by Communist policy-makers allows no part whatsoever for the United States to play in Asia. This vision has been expounded with enthusiasm and pursued, where possible, with vigor, however prudent. The total character of this radical exclusion, this fundamental assault on a vision of balanced power, is not the invention of American observers, nor is a hostile response to it by the United States unreasonable. To this extent, the doctrine of "containment" is valid.

Nevertheless, this doctrine has not proved adequate as a policy, for two interrelated reasons. The first reason is that the abilities of Communist governments and parties are in no way commensurate with their vision. The second reason is that this Communist vision is not by any means the only source of political change in Asia. Many other dynamic forces, customarily lumped together under the name of nationalism, have roles to play. These various forces, which are the motives for many particular visions of the future, result in political changes, which tend to work for greater autonomy of groups and, thus, may work to reduce U.S. influence in some, but not all, cases. Containment, as an aspiration, is inadequate in that it leads to confusion between the impact of these particular national forces and the influence of Communism.

Distinguishing between "nationalism" and "Communism" is not always a simple matter, however, because the Communist strategy of "national liberation" deliberately seeks to confuse and combine them. Moreover, when national forces focus on exclusion of U.S. influence, they may find useful Communist allies.

United States policy must seek, in this shaky ground, a

foundation for power in Southeast Asia that can resist the domination of hostile forces. It is the traditional approach of the United States to think of a "community of free nations" as such a foundation, but the unmobilized and shifting character of these Southeast Asian states has so far proved inadequate.

Recently, the notion of regionalism has been brought forward, most significantly by President Richard Nixon, to lend an appearance of innovation to previous conceptions. Yet, any primitive notions of regionalism in Southeast Asia are fraudulent. The sum of instability added to instability is more instability. For regionalism to assume a significance in the relationships of power, the elements of the regional group—the nation-states—must exhibit cohesion, stability, and the capacity for peaceful change. Since the nations of Southeast Asia generally lack these characteristics, the prospects for rapid development of regional cooperation and strength are dim.

Nevertheless, the notion of regional cooperation is an attractive part of a vision of Southeast Asia's future, around which agreement on a variety of specific programs might be organized, particularly if the viability of component states is accepted as the prerequisite of ultimate regional strength.

If we may assume, then, that, in the future, the leaders of Southeast Asian states will probably strive to maintain the autonomy of their nations while still joining in active international relations, what part is it appropriate for the United States to play? Whatever that part may be—the objectives America seeks to attain and the policies, strategies, and means appropriate to them—it will necessarily be consistent with the national interests of both sides.

In this book, I try to unravel a portion of the complex of issues involved in the American position in Southeast Asia. By looking at the relations between the United States and one Southeast Asian country—Thailand—I am offering both an example of the kind of issues and an analysis of one important case. The interests of the United States and Thailand arise from internal and external political forces. Within an adumbration of such forces, this book highlights the linkages among them. By doing this, one can make a plausible assessment of the potentialities for America.

The question of the interests of the United States in Thailand, as well as in Southeast Asia as a whole, is not settled. In fact, it remains severely agitated as a result of the costly and agonizing war in Vietnam. Nevertheless, both the experiences of the past century and the opinions of learned men seem to support the view that the United States has an enduring interest in preventing the domination of Eastern Asia by any single power, certainly by any single hostile power. From the time America became a Pacific power until 1944, the concrete meaning of this interest was expressed in the determination to "maintain the territorial integrity of China," an assertion directed against Russia, France, and Japan at different times and, in the end, implemented in the Pacific war of 1941–45. The upheaval after the defeat of Japan in 1945, particularly the Chinese Revolution and the establishment of new independent states in Southeast Asia, so modified the strategic elements of East Asia that history no longer served well as a guide to policy. In the subsequent two decades, events developed with a speed and violence that severely tested the capacities of foreign-affairs specialists.

In the normal course of thought on national interest, doctrinal principles, more properly called rules of thumb, play a large role. In nineteenth-century Europe, British interests were defined by rules about the statuses of Belgium and Portugal and the relative sizes of national naval forces. In the same period, U.S. interests were defined by the noninvolvement doctrine and the Monroe Doctrine. Similarly, in the period from the end of the last century until 1945, U.S. interests in East Asia were defined by the Open Door Policy in China.

The utility of such rules of thumb depends upon the persistence of political power relationships to which the rules are applied. But when these power relationships are profoundly modified, as happened in East Asia after the defeat of Japan and the consolidation of Communist control of China, such rules no longer serve as guides to action. Thus, we hear no further discussion of the Open Door Policy in China. We are forced back to the abstract statement that "the permanent interest of the United States in Asia is the maintenance of the balance of power."* But such a statement entails no concrete guidance on policy. The core of the problem of U.S. interests in East Asia continues to be China. But China has, because of the Communist revolution, moved from an object position to a subject position in the grammar of political relations. The rule of the Open Door—that no nation shall dominate China —has been shattered. China is now dominated by the Chinese and is, therefore, a threat to America's vital interests.

If the proposition is granted that a balance of power in East Asia is a permanent interest of the United States and if it is further granted that China is now dominated by a power—the Communist Party of China—that is hostile to the United States in principle and practice, it seems to follow that the permanent interest of the United States is to balance the power of China and to prevent Chinese Communist domination of the remainder of East Asia, that is, Korea, Japan, Taiwan, the Philippines, mainland Southeast Asia, and Indonesia. Pursuit of such a balance has been a major aspect of U.S. policy since June, 1950.

But the simplicity of this situation is largely verbal. Difficulties arise in transforming the verbal formulation into a set of policies, strategies, and programs in specific situations.

The record of this search for a balance of power in Southeast Asia has been frustrating and, in the end, agonizing. Power emerges from cooperation among people in a cohesive

* Hans Morgenthau, *In Defense of the National Interest* (New York: Alfred A. Knopf, 1952), p. 6.

community. However, the basis of such a community in Southeast Asia has proved elusive. The flux of nationalism within a framework of putatively independent, but actually weak and unmobilized, states has so far been a hindrance. The American effort—implemented first by bilateral foreign aid, then by treaties both bilateral and, through SEATO, multilateral, and, finally, by intervention, covert and open—has failed to discover or create the requisite community of power.

This is not the appropriate place for a detailed examination of the history of American successes, of which there are many, or failures, of which there are not a few, in Southeast Asia since 1950. The salient problem is, rather, what possibilities remain to the United States as it emerges from the crisis of the Vietnam war; how can it maintain a balance of power while reducing, rather than increasing, costs? Within the present context, the United States must also examine what role Thailand may assume in any future pattern of power. A judgment of that kind depends on an estimate of Thailand's future ability to sustain the cohesion and the capacity for cooperation from which increasing power and wealth may flow. Finally, we need an estimate of the capacity of the United States, if any, to contribute to the processes that are required to enhance cooperation and growth.

I

The United States and Thailand:
The Historical Background

Thailand is one of America's principal allies on the continent of Asia. It is the largest country on the mainland in Southeast Asia. With a population of more than 33 million people, it is the seventh largest country in Asia.*

For centuries, the Thai people have dominated central Southeast Asia and played a leading part in the history of the region. Given a combination of its strategic location, its resourceful people, and its relatively effective government, Thailand is cast as a leading actor in the future events of that troubled part of the world. Southeast Asia is a peninsular projection of the Asian continent, not unlike Europe, but it also includes a great arc of islands that, on its southern edge, brushes Australia. This peninsula and island complex separates the South China Sea—that is, the western Pacific Ocean— from the Indian Ocean. Southeast Asia has been a site of the historical meeting between the Indian and Chinese civilizations. Not surprisingly, it has been known variously as Further India, Little China, and Indochina.

Southeast Asia, no matter how obscure, turbulent, and chaotic, is not a trivial region. Within the area are ten puta-

---

* This ranking does not include the total populations of the politically divided countries Vietnam and Korea. In each case, if the northern and southern parts are added together, the resulting population is greater than Thailand's.

tive sovereign states* with a combined population of 240 million people. Although the resource base of the region is little explored, it is known to contain major sources of surplus food, fiber, rubber, tin, and petroleum, some of which are already being exploited.

But the importance of Southeast Asia to the United States lies not so much in its power and natural wealth as in its weakness and poverty. This situation is a genuine paradox of human affairs. The instability, the abrupt discontinuity, the propensity to violence, and the generalized turbulence are all reflections of social disorganization and political weakness. In our time, wealth flows from the successful mobilization of human and material resources. Poverty is a consequence not only of unequal distribution but also of the inability to mobilize resources. This inability is not a moral fault so much as a historical condition. Given known technology of contraception and material production, it would be possible, in a purely technical sense, to double the standard of living of the world in ten years, if everyone did exactly what he was told to do. This statement, however, is meaningless, except that it directs our attention to the basic obstacles to growth found in the limitations of politics and organization. This condition, however, will change.

The issue facing the United States now, as it has for twenty years, is what influence can America have on this change, and what possibilities and instruments are there for exerting influence? The alliance with Thailand, as well as the war in Vietnam, will determine the answers to these questions.

The struggle to realize conflicting visions of Southeast Asia's future has been wild and, often, bloody. The people there have long been in the throes of profound conflict—conflict with few rules and little system. Their lives and fortunes have

* Union of Burma, Kingdom of Thailand, Kingdom of Laos, Kingdom of Cambodia, Democratic Republic of Vietnam (North), Republic of Vietnam (South), Federation of Malaysia, Singapore, Republic of Indonesia, and Republic of the Philippines.

been dominated by revolution and war because they, their leaders—genuine or self-elected—and their friends share no agreement on what might be a right and appropriate future. Somehow the rest of the world is drawn into this cauldron, willy-nilly. Why is this so?

A century and a half ago, by and large, Southeast Asia was a matter of little more than curiosity to the rest of the world. The Chinese, Indians, Europeans, and Americans carried on minor trade at various points along the coasts. The Dutch had plantations for growing spices and other valuable tropical products in the islands. Buddhist monks, Christian missionaries, and Islamic teachers actively proselytized among the populations. But the little wars and posturings of petty princes and kings were, at best, curiosa for the world outside —and vice versa. In the subsequent fifteen decades, everything changed. The name of the change was empire.

By 1910—the year before the first Chinese revolution, and shortly after the *Entente Cordiale*—the lives of the people of Southeast Asia were dominated by administration in the spirit of Jeremy Bentham, James Mill, and le Comte de Saint-Simon. Britain, the Netherlands, France, and the United States had claimed various territories of the region and had established colonial administrations in each. The colonies were incipient states, modeled after the nation-states of Europe.

The spread of European power into Southeast Asia and throughout the world was an extraordinarily complicated phenomenon. Neither its causes nor its effects can be fully explained to this day. Nevertheless, we can say that certain characteristics of the world today can be explained by the characteristics of nineteenth-century imperialism.

In the nineteenth century, the states of Europe, together with Japan, were being transformed by a complex process of technological and social reordering. The transformation can be described as the mobilization of national resources within a state structure. That was the time of industrial development, the rise of democracy, and the growth of nationalism, all of which were parts of an interrelated process. Industrial development is a mobilization of the classic factors of production—land, labor, and capital—for productive purposes. The guiding principle of that mobilization is a national, community-wide allocation of these resources in relationship to each other. The social effects of this development process are colossal. People become workers; workers become hours of labor, allocated by the clock; hours of labor add up to livelihood, as measured by a cash market.

Organization is everything. Nature is no longer the principal enemy. On the contrary, other people in competing organizations become the enemy. The struggle for life becomes one of group against group, with control or influence over the state—the ultimate organized group—the final symbol of victory. In this manner, one effect of industrialization is democracy; that is, people become involved in politics, and politics becomes concerned with people.

In Europe, contemporarily with industrialization, the democratic concept of the nation-state—a state based on the legitimate right of a community to govern itself—was being developed in the struggle against the church, the legitimists, the feudal aristocracies, and the imperial houses. Men as subjects became men as citizens, who had rights and duties derived from the strength of the state. Not the least of these rights and duties was the obligation to fight for the independence of the nation-state. The ultimate political mobilization was the *levée en masse,* even as the ultimate economic mobilization was industrialism.

This very simplified version of nineteenth-century Europe is recalled here merely to underline the tremendous sources of state power that were released through the mobilization of the energies within those societies. One outcome of the increased power was the spread of European authority and civilization through the world in a "universal" system of order.

This system had some serious conflicts within it, however,

that help to explain the character of its dissolution. One of these conflicts lies in the different principles by which authority is organized in empires, on the one hand, and in nation-states, on the other. In principle, an empire is center-oriented and hierarchical, while a nation-state is boundary-oriented and egalitarian. An empire is glorious in the capital—in Rome or Peking—but vague on the margins. A nation-state is a rational dullness throughout but strong and clear on its borders. In an empire, the forces of coercion dominate the capital and choose the emperor. In a nation, they dominate the frontier and defend the fatherland.

In the nineteenth century, however, European empires were based on nation-states that had extended themselves in recurring fits of absentmindedness. Perhaps it would be too much to say they could not have lasted, but it is true that they did not last.

Let us briefly examine at least some of the historical reasons for the dissolution of these remarkable empires. The foremost cause of their downfall was that they knocked each other out at the center. The wars of 1914–45 simply devastated the metropolitan powers—Britain, Holland, France, Germany, Japan, and so on. More or less contemporary with this exhaustion was the appearance of two super nation-states, the United States and the Soviet Union. Although the historical development of these two superstates was quite distinct, they are similar in their size, and they share in an extreme development of the industrialization, democratization, and mobilization processes invented in Europe. Neither of these superstates cared much for the mixed up national empires of the nineteenth century; both came, in their own ways, to oppose these empires, but their opposition was mutually incompatible. In short, it is a fair estimate of the process, in Southeast Asia at least, to say that the conditions for the dissolution of these empires were created by peoples and events outside of the imperial territories.

But the spread within the imperial system of the notion—

even the principle—of national statehood provided the channels of dissolution. The imperial system was also a colonial system by which rudimentary elements of statehood were transferred to the imperial peoples and territories. A vague political landscape became the multihued maps of our grade-school texts. Certain specified territories were provided with governments that administered certain mobilizations, particularly the extraction of primary resources. But these administrative governments were branches of national governments and did what national governments had to do; that is, they provided communication facilities and education and other services that commenced the nationalizing process. Very quickly, quasi-national leadership groups appeared, which seized the opportunities of the 1940's and 1950's to claim statehood for their putative nations.

From the dissolution of the empires of Southeast Asia have come a number of weak and, with one exception, small states that never existed before and that share a number of characteristics attributable to the shady circumstances of their conception and birth. The characteristics most important to us here are the political aspects of underdevelopment; the reappearance of older, more primitive systems of order, together with their conflicts; and the possibilities and perils of weak states, which exist in a world of conflicting visions of the future.

There are a variety of ways of dealing with underdevelopment. Among them, the one that uses social mobilization as its central concept is the most fruitful in terms of politics because it centers on processes of organization and allocation of resources, including people, in purposive ways. The outcome of such processes is power. Following this idea, we see that those states that are relatively unmobilized are, by definition, underdeveloped.

It is inaccurate to assert that it is the imperial experience that accounts for the unmobilized character of the weak states that emerged from the European empires in Southeast Asia. On the contrary, it would be more just to attribute whatever elements of national mobilization there may be in such states to the imperial experience. The fact remains that the conditions that permitted the leaders of these states to throw off imperial rule were determined by events, particularly the expansion of Japan and the resulting war, which were largely independent of conditions within the states themselves. These states came into being in a substantially unmobilized condition.

This general statement, as well as subsequent ones of a similar order, varies in the accuracy with which it can be applied to, say, the Philippines, North Vietnam, Indonesia, or Laos. But in relation to developed states—even Italy, for example— the statement is sufficiently true to be useful.

The societies within all the states of Southeast Asia have, generally speaking, been peasant and agrarian, with social structures organized along either family, tribal, or village principles, and with the psychological, economic, social, and political behavior and outlook characteristic of such societies. In other words, they are psychologically superstitious, economically underemployed, socially ascriptive, and politically inactive.

A second, and related, aspect of political underdevelopment is the extraordinary importance of leadership. In the process of imperialism, particularly through the effects of imperial education, groups and individuals appeared who were, or claimed to be, national leaders. From among such people came the leadership of the new states. The character of these leaders varies, but the ones who come close to being true national leaders in unmobilized societies are those who exhibit the quality of charisma. These are men who are believed by their followers to embody a superiority of spirit and morale and who—somehow, miraculously—have made power where there was none. At least psychologically, they strike across the barriers of immobility and constitute a focus, if not a means, for further mobilization efforts. Other types of leaders in Southeast Asia are, on the one hand, more or less superficially transformed kings or princes and, on the other, strong men in command of the organized following of limited groups, usually armies.

Because of the unmobilized character of the societies over which these leaders, charismatic or otherwise, preside, their ability to allocate resources is limited. The limits are set by the extent to which administrative organizations are available and responsive to the leaders' direction. The development of administration varies from state to state, and, therefore, the leaderships' power and stability vary also. But the relative weakness of national leaders, as far as the mobilization and allocation of men and resources are concerned, supports a tendency of these leaders to be oriented to external, rather than internal, affairs.

Such an orientation is substantially a matter of self-preservation. Most of the Southeast Asian states are dramatically beset by internal divisions of competing leadership groups. These competitions commonly verge on, and often descend to, violence. Vietnam, Burma, Laos, and Indonesia are all embroiled in internal rebellions of some magnitude. Under such circumstances, external recognition of legitimacy is very important to maintaining a position of leadership.

Moreover, in an age of foreign aid, resources are available from outside a society to supplement those that can be mobilized internally. In the hands of the more sophisticated national leaders, externally provided resources—principally arms, capital, and technical skills—and the influence that accompanies them can be used to contribute to the task of national mobilization.

However, until national mobilization progresses to a condition wherein leaders can dispose of resources commensurate with their aspirations for self-determination, the autonomy of these leaders will continue to be dependent on their ability to manipulate outside forces. Thus, they remain subject to the influence of the more affluent world powers, which can and will supply necessary resources.

At the same time, because of the unresponsive character of the social structures of their societies, the national leaders are faced with a revival of preimperial social forces. The spread of imperial control did not take place in a politically homogeneous medium. The creators of empires built upon local political systems, with their involved patterns of tributary relationships among local princes and chiefs. Local antagonisms and dominions were exploited by imperialists in order to expand imperial influence. Under the empires, particularly under the influence of the colonial administration, these older patterns were suppressed or, at least, flattened out, although some of the institutions and offices were transmuted into agencies of colonialism. The colonial administrations were, for the most part, not locally responsible, looking rather to the homeland for both legitimacy and direction.

With the dissolution of empire and the devolution of authority to quasi-national leaders, there was no pattern of forces to hold these leaders responsible for their actions. Meanwhile, the older patterns of politics tended to reappear. Because the process of national mobilization was partial, at best, and generally incipient, these old patterns, in many cases, cut into the apparent cohesion of the new states. Thus, we hear much of tribal and ethnic conflicts. Often, these old patterns are as much international as national problems.

Laos is an example *par excellence* of these problems. Beyond question, the little kingdom is the most completely nonnational state in Southeast Asia, if not in the world. It has no national economy, no national social structure, and practically no internal commerce, and the only internal transportation system worthy of the designation national is, rather symbolically, that for air travel, which flies over the heads of the population. Under these circumstances, the old pattern of relationships, in which Vietnamese and Thai manipulated the petty princes of the Laos area, came to the surface immediately upon "independence." The only traditional group not present in Laos today is the Burmese, who are struggling to manage the revived complexity of relations among Burmans, Shan, Karen, and others within and around the Union of Burma.

Whatever substance the state of Laos has comes from an international agreement made in Switzerland in 1962 among the world powers and from a "neutralist," tripartite semi-government in Vientiane, kept solvent by a fairly well-administered program of "foreign assistance," sponsored by the United States and manned by Americans, Thai, and Filipinoes. At least a third of the territory of the Kingdom of Laos is administered by a countergovernment supported and encadred by Vietnamese. It is impossible to say to whom the Prime Minister of Laos is responsible, or who is responsible to him.

In this case, we see a poignant and dramatic example of the fundamental significance of Southeast Asia. Weakness and poverty make this part of the world a medium for realizing visions of the future. But there are differences in the medium. Thailand, although weak and poor, is relatively cohesive and enduring.

Modern Thailand, although never a European colony, is as much an outgrowth of nineteenth-century imperialism as any other Southeast Asian state. But the fact that, throughout the era of imperialism, the Kingdom of the Thai was able to maintain substantial autonomy, if not independence, has made a difference.

The present Chakkri dynasty was founded in 1782, in Bangkok. At the height of its power, the dynasty asserted dominion over central Southeast Asia from Dien Bien Phu (in North Vietnam) to Trengganu (in Malaysia) and from Siem Reap (in Cambodia) and Bassac (in southern Laos) to the Salween River (in Burma). At the outer edges of the royal dominion, the peoples were ruled by tributary princes, while, in areas closer to the capital, the rule became increasingly direct. In short, the Kingdom was a loose domain of local rulers each subordinate, in his own way, to Bangkok law and power and obliged to pay tax or tribute on a more or less regular basis. This kind of domain was characteristic of Southeast Asia before the advent of European colonialism. It was the imposition of colonialism on this shifting pattern that created the contemporary map.

The Thai first met European power in the seventeenth century, but it was not until the middle of the nineteenth century that this power became so insistent and threatening that it forced substantial changes in the normal order of Thai life. The threat of European power was embodied for the Thai in attacks on other people. In 1824–26, the British East India Company defeated the Burmese, a traditional enemy of the Thai, and took control of the Tenasserim coast, thereby blocking a principal corridor of Burmese-Thai conflict. During the course of this war, the Thai King signed the first treaty of friendship and commerce with the Company. A similar treaty was signed with a representative of the United States in 1833. But these treaties were ineffective in opening the country, because the King continued to maintain traditional royal monopolies on trade as well as foreign relations.

It was the forced opening of China by Britain and France in 1840–42 that convinced leading Thai that European power demanded effective accommodation. This conviction was not realized, however, until the early 1850's, when the accession of King Mongkut (Rama IV) brought a "modern" administration to power. Beginning with a Siamese-British treaty in 1855, the Thai Kingdom (known then as Siam), by means of so-called unequal treaties, became a part of the developing imperial system.

The essential character of these treaties, which were the least direct form of imperial intervention, lay in two elements: the treaties (1) resigned to the imperial power substantial control, at least by tariffs, over foreign trade and (2) granted extraterritoriality to citizens and "protected persons" of the imperial powers, which meant that such foreigners were subject to the law of the metropolitan power administered by consular courts rather than to local law. Siam accepted these terms in treaties with Britain (1855), France (1856), the United States (1856), Denmark and the Hanseatic Cities (1858), Portugal (1859), Holland (1860), Prussia (1862), and others.

In the 1860's, European imperialism began changing from demands for "free trade," as embodied in the treaties, to expansion of territorial control. This process first affected Siam in 1864, when Bangkok abandoned to France its suzerainty over the Kingdom of Cambodia. Soon thereafter, French adventurers explored the valley of the Mekong River, and, during the next four decades, France forced Siam to relinquish dominion over all territory east of the Mekong, plus two bits on the west bank, and two more Cambodian provinces. In the same period, Britain forced withdrawal of Siamese authority from four states of northern Malaya and from the watershed of the Salween River in eastern Burma. This last agonizing territorial sacrifice was made in 1909, and the outline map of modern Thailand was finished.

These sacrifices were accepted with monumental anguish, approaching, at times, despair, on the part of the Siamese King and his court. We can, however, from our lofty and dispassionate position, see several aspects of the process that contributed to the strength of today's Thailand. First of all, the territorial sacrifices reduced the Kingdom to a compact and homogeneous land. Second, and probably most important, the pressure of imperialism, which affected the Thai rather gradually over a period of time when their government was in a rather flexible and imaginative condition, forced them to bring about internal reform and reconstruction. Between 1873 and 1935, but most importantly between 1892 and 1910, reforming governments changed the Kingdom from a traditional Southeast Asian royal domain to a modern state, patterned initially on colonial lines, but ultimately adopted the model of the European powers themselves. By 1936, Siam was a constitutional monarchy possessing complete legal autonomy within the community of nations.

The experience of imperialism has made the leaders of Thailand alert against any threat to diminish their genuine but limited autonomy. For such a small country such threats are real and plentiful. A government or regime may inquire about such threats: From where or whom will they come, and by what means will they be delivered? The answer to these questions may be slightly complicated by the character of political life of unmobilized societies.

Threats to a government may be classified as being of either domestic or foreign origin. Because the governmental regime of an unmobilized society tends to be autocratic rather than democratic, revolt is a common *domestic* threat. If such a state is, in addition, small, it may also be threatened by *international* wars and invasions. In this age of transformation, unmobilized societies have a potential for revolutionary change that lurks as a unique and cataclysmic threat to their governments.

In Southeast Asia, these types of threats may well become interconnected. Since 1958, the war in Vietnam has exhibited characteristics of revolt, invasion, and revolutionary mobilization—often, all at the same time. For this reason, among others, the war has been difficult to understand. As a matter of fact, if one insists on using language appropriate to one form of threat to describe another, it is even difficult to talk about the events in Vietnam. Incidentally, that is about the only thing the Vietnam conflict has clearly demonstrated.

Following this line of thought, we can see that, in an un-mobilized society, particularly a relatively small one such as Vietnam or Thailand, a clear division between domestic and foreign affairs is not easy to establish. If we examine Thai Government policy from the last half of the nineteenth century through the 1920's, we will find that almost every activity of the state derived from the problem of the "unequal treaties." The abolition of certain ancient customs and practices, such as slavery, as well as the introduction of new approaches to education, legal administration, and provincial administration, were all designed to demonstrate to the imperial nations the capacity and civilization of the Thai Government. Revenue policy was constrained by treaty restrictions on customs duties and modified by foreign, mainly missionary, objections to gambling and opium. Reform and reorganization of the military and police were designed to build some substantial force to protect against external encroachment. This is not to say that no other motives were at work but, rather, that the unequal treaties were the touchstone of choice.

The end of unequal treaties, however, did not free Thailand's government from this mingling of pressing forces from at home and abroad. As the neighboring empires declined and collapsed, the shifting environment became more threatening or, at least, more uncertain than before.

During this involved course of events, the position of the United States in the affairs of Siam, compared to that of other Western powers, was unique. This was so because the active interests of Americans in the country were for the most part only those of Protestant missionaries. From 1856 onward, the attitude of the U.S. Government in Siam, and in the Far East in general, was one of an open door for all. But, in Siam, the lack of active interest put the United States in a particularly neutral position. The kings of Siam, recognizing this as the case, looked to the United States, often without success, as an arbiter among the powers.

As a general policy of employing foreign advisers to assist in government programs was developed, the Siamese throne came to look to Americans as effective foreign-affairs and general advisers. From 1903 until 1926, an American held the post of either foreign or general adviser, or both, to the Thai throne. Moreover, the first treaty to renounce extraterritoriality completely was negotiated with the United States in 1920. It was agreed between these two countries that such a treaty would be useful to Siam as a model when it negotiated with other, more reluctant, powers. It subsequently served that purpose in a series of negotiations in 1925 with all European powers for such treaties. These negotiations were conducted by Francis B. Sayre, an American, as the Minister of the Government of Siam.

The fact that Siam and the United States had so few impinging interests was at the heart of this curious and happy relationship. In fact, one of the difficulties in negotiating the Siamese-American treaty of 1920 was that the United States had such a negligible interest there. At that time, it was a principle of diplomacy that a state should not grant a concession without receiving a comparable concession in return. But, unlike Britain and France, for example, who had many interests, the United States could not develop an appropriate demand on the Thai to receive as compensation for yielding on extraterritoriality. At this juncture, President Woodrow Wilson made the novel proposal that a principled repudiation of extraterritorial rights could be made simply on the basis of justice. Negotiations then proceeded.

Why, then, have American interests in Thailand developed from virtually nothing in 1920 to an intimate alliance for mutual defense in the 1960's? Have the Americans changed? Or has the world changed?

II

The Alliance of the United States
and Thailand

During the decade ending in 1945, Japanese influence and power intruded into Southeast Asia in a spectacular and decisive way. The most dramatic effect was the termination of European empires. The colonies that had been constructed in the nineteenth and early twentieth centuries emerged from the process as independent states. Thailand shared in the experience and faced a change, in terms of the Kingdom's historic problem of protecting its autonomy and independence.

Japan's convulsive effort to found an empire, first in Northeast Asia, then in China, and, finally, in Southeast Asia and the southwestern Pacific, shattered beyond repair the legitimacy and effectiveness of the colonial positions of Europe in these regions.

But Japanese imperial power clashed fatally with the United States. From the ruins appeared new entities: the Republic of Korea, the People's Republic of Korea, the Republic of the Philippines, Vietnam, the Kingdom of Laos, Cambodia, the Union of Burma, the Federation of Malaya, the Republic of Indonesia, and Singapore. The People's Republic of China and the Republic of China, or Taiwan, also emerged from the ruins of war. As a result of the war between them, the United States assumed overwhelming power and responsibility in the entire Pacific Ocean, while Japan was destroyed, resurrected, and reformed into the leading industrial and trading nation in Asia and, in the Pacific, second only to the United States.

These events together constitute an unbelievable upheaval in political relationships. It is not surprising that the peoples involved, including the American people, should have suffered some anxiety in the face of the imponderables of these developments.

Let us look briefly at these changes from the point of view of the Thai Government. The decade of the 1930's was a period of great change in Thai political life. In 1932, a group of young civil officials and military officers carried out a revolution against the absolute monarchy. The result of this revolution was the acceptance by the throne of a parliamentary constitution. This development was followed by a series of conflicts in which the relative political power of persons and factions was tested. By 1938, a government headed by Colonel Phibun Songkhram and based mainly on his control of the army was in command. In the course of Colonel Phibun's rise to power, both the monarchy and the parliament were reduced very nearly to impotence.

Colonel Phibun's regime was characterized by increasingly radical nationalism, directed, at first, toward Chinese residents in the country, some of whom had been there for many generations, and, subsequently, toward European imperialism. Although Thai political life was preoccupied most of the time with internal political struggles, the effort of Japan to enhance its influence in Thailand was not without effect. Japanese opposition to European imperialism and the idea of "Asia for the Asiatics" was in tune with the nationalism of the Thai leadership. The response was not totally sympathetic, however, so the policy of the government was ambiguous among the pressures of Europeans, particularly the British, and the Japanese.

In 1940, after the fall of France, anti-European nationalism won the day. The government of Thailand escalated a border dispute in Cambodia and Laos and demanded satisfaction from France. This conflict grew to be a small war, which, through the mediation of Japan, resulted in Thailand's taking back certain territories from what was then French Indochina. At the same time, Japan was forcing its way into Vietnam.

The movement of Japan into Indochina in 1940 and 1941 was the irritant that aroused the United States to active opposition. At that time, the Roosevelt Administration sought to persuade Japan not to force an expansion of its empire into Southeast Asia. In the middle of 1941, Japan demanded of the French Administration of Indochina the right to advance troops into southern Vietnam. As a result of these demands, the United States Government froze the assets of Japan in the United States. The action led to Japan's decision to attack Pearl Harbor. The interests of Thailand and the United States were drawing closer.

It is unlikely that the Thai Government was able to foresee any more clearly than the United States or Britain the swift advance of Japan into Southeast Asia, which began in December, 1941. Nevertheless, on December 8, the Thai cabinet, after a few hours of confusion, yielded to the *force majeure* in its own territory and granted Japan the right to pass through the territory and to base troops there. These events led to some further shifts of power within Thailand's leadership, and Phibun Songkhram, soon to be a field marshal and "the Leader," assumed undisputed dictatorial power. He led the government to declare war on Britain and the United States and to accept a treaty of alliance with Japan.

Here, indeed, was an odd development from the point of view of the United States: Thailand—a small nation, literally on the other side of the world; a nation with which the United States had had, for a century, slight but consistently friendly relations; a nation with virtually no capacity to do harm or damage to the United States—was offering to be at war with the United States. The situation was so absurd that the Thai Ambassador to the United States felt that it was not only within his rights but also within his power to decline to deliver the declaration of war. The Field Marshal's gambit was refused. From this refusal flowed curious results.

In the shambles of Japan's defeat in 1945, Thailand had but one friend—the United States. Britain, France, the Soviet Union, and China all had their bones to pick. But the United States, casually interested in the preservation of an independent Thailand and in no way eager to see the empires of European powers re-established in Southeast Asia, intervened to protect Thailand's effort to right itself. In the wake of Japan's defeat, this small incident in the events of the Pacific and Asia was but an intimation of the future closeness between Thailand and the United States.

In the postwar period, the position and policies of Thailand were not simple. Thailand emerged from defeat in an anomalous position. Having been allied with the Japanese, Thailand could have been treated as a defeated belligerent. Because of adroit movement, plus support by the United States, Thailand escaped that fate, although it was necessary to amend relations with Britain, France, China, and, in a minor way, the U.S.S.R. With Britain, Thailand agreed to return territories in Burma and Malaya occupied during the war and to deliver substantial supplies of free rice, desperately needed to feed people in Singapore, Hongkong, and other British territories. With France, Thailand had to agree to return not only all the territory in Cambodia and Laos taken after December, 1941, but also what was "won" during 1941. Thailand was required to accord complete diplomatic recognition and representation to the Republic of China for the first time in history, as well as to remove restrictions on the immigration of Chinese. These requirements were of considerable significance because of the very large and rather militant population of overseas Chinese in Bangkok. Finally, recognition of the

U.S.S.R. and abrogation of anti-Communist legislation were required by the U.S.S.R., as a price for admission to the United Nations. Thailand's government was in no position to resist these demands, no matter how bitter they seemed.

Nevertheless, the government of Thailand was, as it had been before and during the war, unsympathetic with any re-establishment of European power in Southeast Asia. Cooperation with Vietminh forces fighting against France in Indochina was established early, and a Vietminh liaison office was set up in Bangkok. Some arms were moved through Thailand to Indochina in 1946 and 1947. Moreover, important political figures in Thailand established very close relations with the leaders of Lao Issara, the party in Laos that was resisting the reimposition of French administration in Vientiane.

Perhaps the most striking effort of the Thai at that time, although one that came to nothing, was the formation of the Southeast Asia League, the first of a series of regional efforts in which Thailand has taken part. This league, in which Vietnamese from the Vietminh, Burmese, and Thai tried to organize for regional cooperation, was based in Bangkok. Important political leaders of Thailand supported it, in the hope that Thailand could assume a role of leadership among the emerging Southeast Asian states. The effort collapsed because of changes in government in Thailand at the end of 1947.

This change of government began a period of political instability that lasted for several years. Among other effects of this instability, the modification of Thailand's foreign policy was profound. This modification came about because of the upheavals in the Southeast Asian region and particularly because of the consolidation of Communist power in China in 1949, the assertion of U.S. interest in the area, and the Korean War. In 1950, Thailand proved to be receptive to American advances.

Contemplate Asia in the postwar years from the American point of view: The United States was occupying Japan, South

Korea, and the Ryukyu Islands, undertaking to reform and reconstruct the lives of these people. In China, which had been expected to share with the United States the administration of peace and harmony in East Asia, there was the chaos of civil war. In the Philippines, there was devastation and the expectation of immediate independence. In Southeast Asia, efforts to re-establish their authority were made by Britain, France, and the Netherlands, all meeting resistance from local leaders with forces of various magnitudes. Everywhere there was physical damage, social disorganization, ill health, minimal production, and financial chaos. The extent of the wreckage was beyond calculation.

The conception of the postwar Far Eastern situation that guided American postwar policy included two fundamental erroneous predictions. The first of these was that a unified and ultimately prosperous China would cooperate with the United States in maintaining order in East Asia. Whether or not a China unified under a government of the Nationalist Party would have cooperated in a friendly fashion with the United States is itself a questionable proposition. This idea became merely academic because of the outcome of the Chinese civil war, in which the Nationalist Government was defeated and driven off the continent by the Chinese Communist Party. The possibility of cooperation between the Communist regime and the United States, contemplated by the United States in 1949 and early 1950, was aborted by the Korean War, which began in June, 1950. Thus, a policy based on the assumption of a friendly China necessarily had to be abandoned.

The second mistaken assumption of U.S. postwar policy was that the European powers would be able to establish an orderly situation in Southeast Asia. It was hoped that they would follow the American example in the Philippines of a supportive relationship toward independent former colonies and that very little U.S. involvement would be required. For various reasons, this also turned out to be a chimera. In fact, it was in Indochina, the Southeast Asian salient into the Pacific, that the assumption proved least accurate.

For reasons of simple economy, the United States abandoned the administration of the immediate postsurrender problems in Southeast Asia to the British command in India. With a few exceptions, notably the American support of Thailand and the American role through the United Nations in Indonesia's struggle with the Netherlands, the United States turned away from the area to attend to Northeast Asia, China, and the Philippines.

These pages are not sufficient to rehearse the turbulent events of the revolutionary civil war in China or the extraordinary triumph of humane endeavor in the occupations of Japan and Korea. But the consequences of these two processes led the United States to return its attentions to the states of Southeast Asia.

By 1950, it was quite clear to the United States that, because of the failure of such fundamental elements of policy, it would be necessary to reorganize the American position in order to forestall the development of a hostile bloc in East Asia. This reassessment of policy, which was under way by early 1950, was confirmed and accelerated by the Korean War.

The security concerns of Thailand, however, unlike those of the United States, tend to be local and immediate. Four states border on the Kingdom. Burma, on the west and north, and Malaysia, on the south, have displayed their moments of tension. Since 1948, however, the northeastern and eastern frontiers with Laos and Cambodia, respectively, have been the locations of events and origins of trends producing deep anxiety and concern over foreign affairs. The sympathy for independence efforts in Laos, Cambodia, and Vietnam that was shown by Thai leaders in the early postwar years was transformed by the increasing role of hostile, Communist-led forces in these efforts. The intrusion of the power of Communist leadership has accelerated Thailand's quest for security through arrangements with great powers.

Since 1950, the United States has been central to this quest. In that year, the decision to move in this direction was signaled by Thailand's recognition of the Bao Dai Government of Vietnam, as well as the governments of semi-independent Cambodia and Laos. This decision was not undisputed in Bangkok and, in fact, resulted in a Foreign Minister's resignation. It was, indeed, a pregnant decision because it signified an intention, subsequently fulfilled, to gain the protection of the United States against Communist-led power. It initiated a course of events that has since resulted in an effective bilateral defensive alliance between Thailand and the United States, as well as the basing of American forces in Thailand. This course of events has not been without its difficulties over the years.

How did Thailand view this foreign-policy problem between 1950 and 1970? In some ultimate way, Thailand is devoted to the notion of collective security. As is appropriate to a small state, Thailand judges international organizations on the basis of whether they provide assurance that its position as an independent state will be given at least minimal support by other states as a matter of common self-interest. Thailand's participation in the United Nations, including a small contribution of troops in Korea and the provision of facilities for the U.N. Economic Commission for Asia and the Far East (ECAFE) and other international agencies in Bangkok, is a token of the government's earnestness about supporting these efforts. Small states, unlike great powers, increase their prestige and security through the United Nations. In effect, the organization accredits these states and provides a public forum in which they can assert their claims. The leaders of the Thai governments have perceived this fact and have acted in accordance with it. Nevertheless, as statesmen descending from a tradition of authentic responsibility, Thai leaders are not misled by the rhetoric of United Nations–based collective security. In general, they do not accept the idea that foreign affairs are suspectible to simple legal manipulation. They have consistently sought security through more specific and tangible means.

From the point of view of Thailand, the world consists mainly of the Southeast Asian and Pacific states, including the United States, as well as funds for financial and technological aid provided by such organizations as the International Bank for Reconstruction and Development (IBRD), the Colombo Plan, the Asian Development Bank (ADB), and by bilateral aid programs. The rise of Communist power in China, power that has addressed itself to Thailand in a set of attitudes ranging from openly hostile to skeptically conversational, has modified this world greatly for the Thai. Insofar as China has been hostile to the Thai Government, the Thai leaders have sought support from outside the region, particularly from the United States. At the same time, certain Thai leaders have also permitted themselves to explore the possibilities of hedging, by informal contacts with China. The complete story of these explorations in the mid-1950's is still not publicly known, but, because of internal changes in Thailand (for example, the Sarit coup of 1957–58) and a simultaneous hardening of Chinese attitudes, they appear to have had no lasting result. In any case, the Thai Government views the People's Republic of China as a powerful threat, although not necessarily an immediate one, to the continuing existence of the Kingdom of Thailand.

After the consolidation of Communist power in China, the United States sought to reorganize its Asian and Pacific position on a new basis. The foundations of the new policy were to be Japan and Southeast Asia. Negotiations for a Japanese peace treaty went forward simultaneously with exploratory offers of friendship and assistance to nations in Southeast Asia. Thailand responded favorably to this new American policy, and, in 1950, the relationship between these two countries entered a course that has brought them into greater and greater involvement with each other. The expanding concern of the United States in Southeast Asia converged with Thailand's alarm at hostile Communist power in China and Vietnam. It was the persuasion of the American Government, based on assurances of assistance, although not of any alliance (the American Ambassador stated that "This agreement is not a military alliance nor is it a defense pact"),* that led the Thai Government, over some domestic opposition, to recognize the Bao Dai Government of Vietnam in late February, 1950. This act was followed by recognition of South Korea in March. Later in the year, agreements between Thailand and the United States for educational exchange, economic and technical cooperation, and military assistance were signed. During the course of the negotiation of these agreements, the outbreak of the Korean War stilled opposition to a closer relationship with the United States. Thailand quickly sent both rice and troops to Korea.

The government of Thailand became increasingly concerned about events in Vietnam and Laos in the subsequent few years. It feared Vietnamese expansion toward or into the valley of the Mekong, as well as subversive activities among Thai-Lao and Vietnamese living in the northeastern region of the country, facing Laos. Such fears were enlivened by Vietminh military thrusts to the Mekong River in 1953 and by the loss of Dien Bien Phu in 1954. (Dien Bien Phu, which is ethnically a Thai town, was once tributary to Bangkok. It also is a strategic gate to Laos from North Vietnam, which is why the French chose to defend it.) These events and the collapse of France's ability to resist the Vietminh made the Thai Government seek a firmer American commitment. Thus, when the United States started exploring the possibilities of a

* *The Department of State Bulletin,* vol. XXIII, no. 591, October 30, 1950, p. 702.

treaty for collective defense in Southeast Asia, Thailand responded eagerly. The outcome was the Manila Pact and the Southeast Asia Treaty Organization (SEATO), which is headquartered in Bangkok.

In the drafting of the Manila Pact, Thailand favored including South Vietnam, Cambodia, and Laos in the treaty area. The Thai Government also sought a strong clause on subversion. It was disappointed in the final draft, which it felt was equivocal. Nevertheless, Thailand took considerable satisfaction in the commitment of the United States to undertake the defense of Thailand against Communist aggression. This satisfaction was moderated by American reluctance to commit troops or to establish a military command structure in the organization.

In the years since the establishment of SEATO, the relationship between the United States and Thailand has been troubled by recurring crises of confidence, arising from both parties' skepticism about the firmness of the commitment. These crises have been resolved by increasing the amount of involvement. A brief look at the history of these crises should cast some light on the character of the relationship.

SEATO was established as one of a number of responses to the 1954 settlement of the war between France and the Vietminh in Vietnam. Two other responses—the adoption by India and Indonesia of a neutral posture in regard to the divisions between the Communist powers and the West, and Communist China's acceptance of a policy of "peaceful coexistence," focused on the slogans of the Bandung Conference in 1955, "Afro-Asian solidarity" and the "spirit of Bandung"—resulted in a potentially anti-American environment in Asia. Under these banners, Communist China sought to oust American influence from Southeast Asia largely by enticement rather than threat. This policy of China's was intended to disprove the assumption of Communist aggression upon which SEATO was based, while providing an incentive to small

Asian countries, including Thailand, to reduce involvement with the United States.

Simultaneously, the political life of Thailand took a curious turn. The leaders of the government, for reasons of their own, reversed their policy of restraint and repression. They sought, by liberalization, to put themselves on a basis of support through popular elections. In fact, their popular base was limited, and very widespread criticism of their policies and themselves emerged in the election process. The slogans "Afro-Asian solidarity," "the spirit of Bandung," and "peaceful coexistence" served as one major theme of criticism. Thus, confidence in the political base for SEATO in Thailand was shaken both among the leaders of Thailand and other member states, including the United States.

But the spirit of Bandung was working on the United States as well. Tension over the Taiwan Straits after 1950 led to the brink of war in 1958 but then suddenly de-escalated into the first direct talks between Communist China and the United States. This apparently conciliatory tendency between the two giants caused alarm among Thai leaders, who now questioned the strength of the American commitment to resist the expanding Chinese influence in Southeast Asia. Thus, in its first years, the serious character of SEATO was widely doubted.

Relations between the United States and China blew hot and cold between 1955 and 1958. Despite the easing of the crisis in U.S.-Chinese relations in the late summer of 1958, however, the pattern of events both within Thailand and abroad, from which doubts had arisen, changed sharply in 1958. During that year, China began moving away from its drive for peaceful coexistence and in the direction of a harder line toward Thailand and other countries. Within the Kingdom, a *coup d'état* led by Field Marshal Sarit Thanarat established a new "revolutionary" regime that definitely terminated the period of free criticism of government policy. The regime's motives were complicated. They showed an awareness of the close connection between foreign politics and domestic politics. Simultaneous criticism of the previous government's close association with the United States and the more or less *sub rosa* explorations by certain departed leaders of a possible Chinese *détente* played a salient role in public explanations of the regime's overthrow.

In addition, during 1958, tension between Thailand and Cambodia reached explosive proportions when Cambodia extended *de jure* recognition to Communist China. Unprecedented public demonstrations in Bangkok and some alarm in the Thai Government followed the Chinese-Cambodian communiqué, which included hostile allusions to Thailand. These events abroad, combined with a minor financial crisis and continuing neutralist and even Maoist criticism of the government's foreign policy, led the coup group to suppress constitutional government.

After taking power, the new regime reaffirmed its commitment to the United States. But it was put on a "new" basis—that of pursuing an "independent" foreign policy. This verbal trick permitted Field Marshal Sarit to adhere to his demand for a free policy, while continuing to rely on American protection. It was argued that the situation required Thailand "freely" to associate itself with American protection.

A crisis in Laos that began in 1959 and was not settled until 1962 was a direct challenge to the validity of SEATO as a basis for U.S.-Thai relations. During 1957 and 1958, both of these countries had been encouraging the government of Laos to take a more forthright, rigorously anti-Communist stance. The fragility of the Lao Government's position was revealed in 1959, when it was suddenly overthrown by a relatively obscure army officer. This *coup d'état* plunged the political factions of Laos into a civil war that quickly attracted the intervention of North Vietnam, Thailand, Communist China, the Soviet Union, and the United States.

The government of Thailand backed the so-called right-wing faction in this war, fearing a replication of the hostile neutrality of Cambodia. Moreover, Thailand sought the intervention of SEATO to prevent any expansion of Communist influence in the Lao Kingdom. SEATO proved incapable of combined action beyond verbal protestations, and, in the end, only certain members—the United States, the United Kingdom, Australia, and New Zealand—were able to respond. SEATO's internal disunity alarmed and disillusioned Thailand, whose Prime Minister said to the SEATO ministers in 1961, "Instead of setting about our work in complete unison, we have before us a sad spectacle of filibustering, contention, and working at cross-purposes."*

The United States, faced with the distasteful prospect of a confrontation with China and the Soviet Union in the remote, jungle-covered mountains of Laos, was short on enthusiasm. The administration of President John F. Kennedy finally rejected the possibility and set about negotiating an international agreement to neutralize Laos.

Thailand was in a dilemma. On one hand, SEATO had demonstrated that it would not work in Laos, but, on the other hand, the treaty embodied a commitment from the United States to defend the Kingdom of Thailand. What was the value of this commitment? How could it be made to work?

By ingenious effort, Thailand succeeded in disposing of the water and keeping the baby when its Foreign Minister, Thanat Khoman, and U.S. Secretary of State Dean Rusk announced in 1962 that "the United States regards the preservation of the independence and integrity of Thailand as vital to the national interest of the United States and to world peace." In addition, it was declared that "the United States intends to give full effect to its obligations under the [SEATO] Treaty to act to meet the common danger in ac-

* Thailand, Ministry of Foreign Affairs, *Foreign Affairs Bulletin,* August-September, 1961.

cordance with its constitutional processes. The Secretary of State reaffirmed that this obligation of the United States does not depend upon the prior agreement of all other parties to the treaty, since this Treaty obligation is individual as well as collective."*

By this declaration, the interests of Thailand and those of the United States became fully congruent on the matter of the defense of Thailand's independence and territorial integrity, including defense against subversion by Communists. In the years since 1962, the two countries have worked together much more closely in devising strategy, plans, and programs regarding the Mekong frontier.

Declining fortunes in South Vietnam during 1964 shifted the stress of U.S.-Thai relations. Until that time, the difficulty arose from Thai skepticism about U.S. willingness to implement the defensive commitment. But, following the decision to use air power against North Vietnam, the United States sought air bases in Thailand. Thus, the shoes suddenly turned up on the other foot. The government of Thailand was being asked to make an active contribution to the prosecution of war against North Vietnam by permitting basing of America's principal attack force on its territory. Thailand proved willing, six major air bases were constructed by the United States, and, eventually, about 50,000 U.S. military personnel were stationed in Thailand. It is reported that most of the sorties against North Vietnam in 1966, 1967, and 1968 were flown from these bases in Thailand. Bombing of North Vietnamese facilities in Laos, as well as attacks in South Vietnam, also have originated in Thailand. Some confusion surrounds these developments because, for months after the bases had become an open secret in 1965, the two governments continued to deny their existence. Ultimately, under pressure from the

* *The Department of State Bulletin,* vol. XLVI, no. 1187, March 24, 1962, p. 498.

American press, they were acknowledged by both sides and Thailand's commitment to assist the United States and its other allies in Vietnam was official.

The U.S. forces in Thailand, of which perhaps 90 per cent are air-force contingents, are engaged in prosecuting the Vietnam war by bombing. In short, they are not part of U.S. involvement either in defense of Thailand from direct invasion or in efforts to control actual or incipient insurrection in the country. Of the 50,000 U.S. troops, as many as 2,500 may be engaged in efforts designed to strengthen the Thai military capability, through either training activities or construction of logistical facilities.

In 1967, this commitment of bases was supplemented in a significant way by Thailand's agreement to send a ground-force contribution to South Vietnam. Thai troops began arriving in 1968, and their number has risen to a total of 12,000 infantry and support troops. The Thai Government considers them a symbol of its earnestness in the defense of the Kingdom from Communist-led power.

So, in the 1960's, Thailand and the United States came to be allied. Both allies have devoted resources and lives to the common cause, and the character of the relationship has, therefore, changed, giving rise to a deeper and more complex set of problems.

In Thailand, in its government and among the public, there is anxiety about having moved so close to the fire. While the investment of the United States in Southeast Asian defense is much greater than before, Thailand has also laid more on the line. Therefore, the ability of the United States to pursue the effort to a satisfactory conclusion—an ability measured by both political will and the capability actually to implement such an end—is of much greater importance.

At the same time, the U.S. Government has been alarmed by events in remote parts of Thailand that could be interpreted as an incipient rural rebellion. Washington is haunted by a specter of Thailand, the base area and ally, crumbling into a state of chaos and violence, becoming another expensive and frustrating liability comparable to South Vietnam. So the alliance continues to be tense and anxious.

III

Thailand's Security Policy

The Role of the United States

The United States is Thailand's biggest foreign-policy problem. The interests of the two countries are convergent but by no means permanently congruent. In fact, they may suddenly diverge in significant ways. At the same time, the closeness of the alliance between the two and the resulting high level of activity make the United States a difficult exercise in diplomatic management for Thailand.

The salient elements of Thailand's foreign policy are the alliance with the United States, active foreign trade and economic relations, and participation in limited regional groupings, as well as in the United Nations and other, more specialized, international organizations. As the next chapter will show, a number of internal policies aimed toward assimilation, mobilization, and integration of various segments of society are connected with foreign influences. These policies derive in part from fear of hostile forces in East Asia, principally the Chinese and Vietnamese Communist governments; concern about subversion from abroad; ambition for economic growth; and desire for greater regional stability and cooperation.

The Thai Government has pursued these policies independently while, at the same time, consistently seeking U.S. participation and support. Thailand's effort to encourage an active role for the United States has met with success, but the success has not resulted entirely from Bangkok's own doing. Moreover, a more active role for the United States in Thailand's foreign affairs has not failed to develop its own problems. The character of these problems can be summarized under four headings: (1) the economic question, (2) the question of overpresence, (3) the reliability question, and (4) the insurance question.

Economically, Thailand and the United States compete in the world's markets for several commodities, particularly rice and feed grain. The United States is also a market for various Thai products. The currency of Thailand is closely tied to the dollar, because its main reserves, worth more than $1 billion, are held in U.S. Treasury bonds. Therefore, the policies of the United States serve as an important foundation for Thailand's economic position. Diverging economic interests of the two countries have been managed effectively up to now, and security considerations have submerged the significance of potential or actual conflicts.

The amount, however, of U.S. involvement in Thailand has increased steadily in recent years. Since the great intervention by U.S. forces began in Vietnam in 1965, large numbers of American military men fighting in Vietnam either have been based in Thailand or visited there. The number of Americans involved in assistance for Thailand and in other business activities has also risen. United States spending, both military and economic, public and private, has made an important contribution to Thai economic growth. All these American activities are a focus for ambivalent attitudes of anxiety, disgust, and greed among the Thai that sometimes erupt as hostility toward the U.S. presence. Editorials have sounded the alarm against the corruption of Thai culture and morals by the American presence.

The Thai feel this way, in part, because of their nostalgic reaction against the social effects of urbanization, but the feeling is reinforced by the residual fear that the United States may, in the end, be an unreliable ally. Thai leaders, as well as the public, are not unconscious of the fact that the U.S. involvement in Southeast Asia has been recent, reluctant, and hesitant. Controversy in the United States about this involvement is lively enough to attract the notice of the Thai and arouse their concern.

Thai leaders know that the interests of the United States and Thailand can easily diverge. A precipitous withdrawal from Vietnam, abandonment of support for a friendly Laos, support for Cambodia, or even some reconciliation with China can all be seen as possibilities in the near or distant future. Any one of these developments would embarrass, and some would defeat, Thailand's present policies. Therefore, the question of reliability is of no little consequence.

Uneasiness about it is stimulated further by the clear-cut commitment Thailand has made to a pro-American, anti-Communist policy. Some writers, citing Thailand's experience with Japan and the United States during World War II, have attributed to Thailand a foreign "policy of insurance."* By this, they refer to the fact that, having made a commitment to Japan in 1941, Thailand also maintained contacts with the United States. But it is more appropriate to call "insurance" an approach to foreign relations rather than a policy. It is an approach long honored in Southeast Asia, if not the whole world. It is based on the twin assumptions that neighbors are ambitious and allies are unreliable. The approach dictates that, if caught between two large powers in conflict, one must join and rely on the stronger. But, because situations change and because judgments can be faulty and friends fickle, the best way to insure safety is by keeping open, as far as possible, lines of retreat to the other camp. The ideological intransigence of the present conflict between the United States and China in South-

* For example, see M. Kosaka, "Southeast Asia and the Powers," in *Japan's Future in Southeast Asia* (Kyoto, Japan: Center for Southeast Asian Studies, Symposium Series II, 1966), p. 86.

east Asia makes any such approach difficult to effect. States in a time of ideological conflict are not interchangeable and cannot be shifted from one side to the other without great upheaval. The diminution of insurance possibilities stimulates anxiety about commitments to an ally and concern about that ally's reliability. Nevertheless, in spite of the risks, Thailand's pursuit of security remains based on its alliance with the United States.

Security means maintaining national independence and the integrity of the Kingdom. Thailand's limited capacity to mobilize its human and material resources constrains the country's ability dynamically to pursue autonomous and coherent external objectives. In fact, its security policy is largely responsive to both internal and external events, so it is difficult to induce, from historical evidence, a concise definition of the character and objectives of this policy.

Nevertheless, there are some consistent imperatives of Thailand's policy. One of these, practiced for decades, has been to keep to a minimum the influence of foreign power and to maintain the maximum degree of autonomy for Thai leaders.

It is also an imperative that national integrity be maintained. Thailand's integrity involves, at least, the preservation of the three basic institutions of Thai society, namely, the monarchy, the Buddhist religion, and the nation. In recent years, these imperatives have been explicated in a nationalist pseudo-ideology called Thai-ism.

Thailand's Security Problems

Since 1950, Thailand has pursued a fundamentally conservative policy in the world and in Southeast Asia. It appears that, after the period 1946–48, marked by flirtation with the movements resisting the re-establishment of European imperialism, the government concluded that European imperialism, in pre–World War II form in any case, was no longer a significant threat to the Kingdom's autonomy. It also seems to have concluded that Communist power, particularly in China and Vietnam, threatened to gain control over the chaotic situation following the war and that the success of that enterprise would have been a threat to Thailand's national integrity. The revision of world order that is implied in the Communist vision of the future was too radical and too indigestible. Thus, Thailand's security policy has been strongly opposed to Communist expansion and generally consistent with the trend of Western, particularly American, policy.

Because of the contingencies of Thailand's geographical and strategic position, as well as the limitations of the Kingdom's own capacities, elements of security policy have had their own unique character. As previously mentioned, these elements can be broken down into several categories: (1) the defense against possible invasion, (2) the quest for regional stability, (3) the promotion of domestic development and prosperity through foreign economic relations, and (4) the defense against potential or actual subversion. These categories are interrelated by persistent attention to defending the Kingdom's independence and integrity.

Thailand's main concern about invasion has centered on the Lao frontier. Laos was created by France, which arbitrarily defined its territory by drawing borders along certain mountain ridges and river banks at a time when jurisdictions in the area were vague. The government of the Kingdom of Laos, after 1940, was an amalgamation of Mekong River principalities under the "protection" of France. In that guise, Laos was a part of French Indochina, in its various forms, until the dissolution of that entity by several agreements in 1954. Its population, estimated at 2 to 3 million, is ethnically varied. The Lao are a dialect group of the Thai-speaking peoples, and they share many fundamental social and economic patterns with the people of Thailand. They are a riverine people, cultivating rice in flooded fields. They practice

Buddhism in the Thai style and share shrines in the valley of the Mekong with people from Thailand. Their social and political history is of a piece with that of the other Thai people. The three main principalities of Laos—Luang Prabang, Vientiane, and Champassak—participated in the contentious history of central Southeast Asia. The mountainous areas of Laos are thinly populated by a variety of upland people, some of whom speak the Thai dialects.

The present character of Lao politics is an outgrowth of the dissolution and aftermath of French hegemony in Indochina. The leaders of Laos, particularly the brothers Prince Souvanna Phouma, present Prime Minister, and Prince Souphanouvong, leader of the Communist Pathet Lao, played their part in that intricate drama, which, of course, included the Vietnamese and Cambodians as well.

In the years since the French withdrawal from Laos in 1954–55, control over Laos has been a dispute among the Vietnamese Northeast, the Thai Southwest, and the Lao of the middle Mekong. From the point of view of Thailand, the territory of Laos is an unstable frontier, shifting with the forces of East Asia, both Vietnamese and Chinese.

Insofar as invasion has been considered a genuine threat, it has been assumed that it will come from either China or Vietnam through Laos. The instability of conditions in Laos and operations of Vietnamese troops there, which on more than one occasion in recent years actually reached the east bank of the Mekong, have lent a degree of credibility to such a threat. Thailand's interest in a defense pact with the United States, which was realized in SEATO, arose from the fear of such a contingency. SEATO planning and exercises have focused on the possibility of invasion.

The international settlement of the Laos question in 1962 (see pages 38–40) has deteriorated under pressure of the war in Vietnam. That agreement asserted that Laos would remain neutral among the contending parties in the region. This neutrality was to have been implemented by a coalition government constituted of representatives of the three recognized factions among the Lao—the left-wing Pathet Lao, the neutralists, and the right-wing southern faction. Each faction was to have its own armed forces. The neutral coalition did not survive. The issues that occasioned its dissolution had to do with integration of armed forces. The mutual suspicion about the external backers of each group were insurmountable. The Pathet Lao movement has been closely linked to North Vietnam since at least 1950, and a rather clear link between the right-wing Forces Armées Royales (FAR) and the government of Thailand emerged in the period 1960–63. As the coalition went to pieces, the neutral army lost any ability to sustain itself and also dissolved. Since 1963, Laos has been plagued by low-level warfare and intervention from North Vietnam, China, and Thailand.

A strategy for dealing with the Lao frontier problem that is satisfactory to Thailand has been difficult to develop in concert with SEATO or even with the United States. The issues lie in the different values of a forward defense and a river defense. Thailand prefers to plan forward-defensive actions designed to hold the entire valley of the Mekong and prevent or minimize fighting in Thai territory. The conflicting view is to begin defense at the river and to hold there or fall back into northeastern Thailand if necessary.

The threat is ambiguous. In northwestern Laos, China has been active from time to time in constructing roads from Yunnan Province. These roads appear to be designed to connect Southwest China and North Vietnam while they provide access to the remote reaches of the Lao frontier from those two areas. Along the frontier with Vietnam in the east, roads have also been built to enlarge the capacity of the so-called Ho Chi Minh Trail from North to South Vietnam.

Because the difficulty of transport has made any invasion of Thailand through Laos seem rather unlikely, these roads have an unsettling tendency. Nevertheless, the threat of such an invasion continues to be rather improbable. The obviously repulsive character of the American strategy of falling back is mitigated by the unlikely character of the threat in the first place.

Thailand's approach to the problem of the Mekong has led to a profound interest in the politics of Laos. The degree of Thai intervention in Lao politics is difficult to assess, but there certainly has been more than is publicly conceded. The relationships between some principals of Lao politics and Thai political leaders are, no doubt, very close, and Thai money, personnel, and, probably, forces have certainly played a part in Lao political events. Nevertheless, Thailand has modified its policy of the period from 1954–61, which dictated that Laos must have a clearly anti-Communist government. Since 1962, Thailand's government has accepted the notion, however unreal, of a neutral Laos guaranteed by international agreement and has cooperated with the government of Prince Souvanna Phouma, an avowed neutralist. The modification was contingent upon a clear and concrete assurance by the United States of its willingness to defend the independence and integrity of Thailand in the Lao area.

The government of Thailand has also been worried from time to time about border incursions, if not invasion, from Cambodia. The relationship between these two countries is quite different from that between Thailand and Laos. Cambodia is an ancient and self-conscious state pressed and pursued for centuries from two sides by the Vietnamese as well as the Thai. Like that of Laos, its continued existence as a separate state is problematical, but the response of the Cambodian Government is different.

Prince Norodom Sihanouk, the Cambodian chief of state, has proved an ingenious, if disingenuous, diplomatic manipulator whose program has been a loud and persistent reiteration of Cambodia's claim to existence. He has depicted himself as the leader of a small, virtually helpless, state that is the political object of aggrandizement and domination by several powers—Vietnam, Thailand, the United States, and, probably, China.

As the first Indochina war reached its climax in 1953–54, Prince Sihanouk vainly sought support from Thailand for Cambodia's independence and security. At the Geneva Conference in 1954, his delegates made eleventh-hour demands that prevented a division of Cambodia and permitted a wide latitude for diplomatic activities. This triumph of bargaining created conditions favorable to the talents for maneuver so brilliantly displayed by the Cambodian prince.

Subsequently, Prince Sihanouk has sought effective insurance. In 1958, he recognized the People's Republic of China. This move created consternation in Bangkok and precipitated a decade of embittered and hostile relations between Thailand and Cambodia. Border incidents, not a few of which have involved brief fire fights and some casualties, have occurred frequently. These have led to mutual fear, which, in the case of Thailand, has been encouraged by Cambodia's opening to Peking. Thailand professes to see this as another Communist threat in Southeast Asia and one that is directed toward Thailand. Thailand has tried to alert the United States to the threat it perceives in Cambodia, but with little success, because the United States has not regarded Cambodia as an authentic source of Communist menace to U.S. interests in the area. Nevertheless, Thailand abhors Cambodia's determined neutralism, while Cambodia views Thailand as a threat to its independence and integrity.

Beyond Laos and Cambodia lies Vietnam. The historical relationship between the Thai people, particularly those in the central plain of Thailand, and the Vietnamese is one of competition for territory and suzerainty, especially in Laos and Cambodia. The early intricacies of this story need not concern us here. Since 1950, when the government of Thailand recognized the Bao Dai Government of Vietnam, Thailand has played an active role in resisting the expansive Vietnamese efforts energized by the Communist leadership in both Vietnams. The highlights of this resistance have been participation in SEATO, support for the anti-Vietnamese factions in Laos, and the provision of Thai troops and bases for U.S. forces engaged in the Vietnam war.

Regardless of whether Thailand's position on Vietnam is interpreted as resistance to East Asian culture, to Chinese influence, to Communist domination, or, simply, to Vietnam, the trend is an historical one and remains clear today. For this reason, the proposition that Thailand's concern arises merely from a "clientele" relationship with the United States is a dubious one. The competition, if not conflict, between the two peoples is fundamental to the political life of mainland Southeast Asia and, therefore, to the permanent security considerations of Thailand.

Foreign Economic Policy

Thailand's policy on foreign trade and economic relations was established on a conservative basis seventy-five years ago. Its two basic principles are promotion of primary exports—rice, rubber, tin, feed grain, fibers, and so forth—and maintenance of fiscal stability and good credit. Since World War II, the implementation of this policy has developed a degree of sophistication aimed at inducing internal economic growth.

Basically, the government of Thailand assumes the Kingdom to be economically as well as politically a participant in a world system. Never in modern times has any government of Thailand sought economic autarchy. On the contrary, all policies have been designed to facilitate trade and, recently, to encourage foreign investment. The government has been an active borrower for investment purposes, accepting loans mainly from other governments and international banks.

The shift of economic policy toward a basic concern with growth, in contrast to simple stability, is part of a long-run shift of attention from almost purely international concerns to a direct response to internal political forces.

Regional Problems

Instability in Southeast Asia is a general threat to the integrity of Thailand. The conflicts and confrontations among peoples and states of the region, whether in Indochina or within the Malay Barrier (Malaysia, Indonesia, and the Philippines), all work to Thailand's disadvantage both politically and economically. Consequently, Thailand has sought a role in easing tensions and developing organizations to cope with these problems.

Thailand's first flirtation with regionalism was in the years immediately after World War II. Southeast Asia was a chaos of conflicting forces and tendencies through which ran the thread of opposition to European imperialism. In 1947, a group of political leaders from Burma, Thailand, and Vietnam announced the establishment of an organization called the Southeast Asia League. The purpose of the League was to find a structure for organized cooperation in the resistance to a return of French or British colonialism. Although there was no official Thai Government participation, leading figures of the time supported the cause. Events in the participating countries, including a *coup d'état* in Thailand, overtook the infant effort, and it died.

It was not until the middle of the next decade that new attempts were made to find a mode of regional cooperation. These attempts were dominated by the cold-war character of world politics. Two approaches emerged in the area. One approach involved the defensive SEATO alliance, which was a response to the final collapse of French imperialism in Indochina. As we have seen, Thailand played a leading role in setting up SEATO. The second approach was initiated by a group of Asian powers—principally India and Indonesia—that wished to find a middle road in the bipolar world of that time. This effort, which was ultimately supported by Communist China, resulted in the Conference of Afro-Asian Nations convened in Bandung, Indonesia, in 1955.

The government of Thailand, with some reluctance, joined the Bandung Conference, which marked the high point of cold-war neutralism. At the conference, Thailand's Foreign Minister discussed various points at issue between Thailand and the Communist governments of North Vietnam and China. These discussions were the first moves in a brief exploration by various elements of the Thai political scene of the possibilities, if any, of better relations with Asian Communist governments. The results of these explorations appear to have been negligible. Moreover, the grandiose vision of a regionalism of all of Asia and Africa could never be realized. It passed with the heroes of the new, emerging forces —Sukarno, Nkrumah, and Nehru.

The quest for regional cooperation in Southeast Asia entered a new phase in 1961, with the formation of the Association of Southeast Asia (ASA) by three smaller nations—Thailand, the Philippines, and Malaya. The launching of ASA marked the first effort since the abortive Southeast Asia League to find a basis of power in the cooperation of Southeast Asian states. The Foreign Minister of Thailand has played a leading role in the effort.

ASA, in its early years, worked for cooperation at a low level in dealing with low-level technical problems and demonstrated a capacity for agreement commensurate with the limited capacities of the member states. It inevitably and properly became involved not only in disputes between two of its members—the Philippines and Malaya—over North Borneo but also in the almost catastrophic death throes of Sukarno's government in Indonesia. The burden of these problems

rested on traditional diplomacy, in which Thailand participated actively, rather than on ASA as an organization. The
notion behind ASA revealed a striking resilience in the face
of these conflicts and survived the break of relations between
the two members and also the confrontation between Indonesia and Malaysia. When the confrontation had ended and
Indonesia had entered a new foreign-policy course, the idea of
a limited regional organization became the focus of wider
cooperation.

In 1966 and 1967, again with Thailand taking a leading
role, a new, larger-scale organization was developed. Although
efforts to attract the participation of Burma and Cambodia
were fruitless, a conference in Bangkok in 1967 announced
the formation of the Association of Southeast Asian Nations
(ASEAN). The members were the three ASA nations plus
Singapore and Indonesia. Subsequently, ASA and ASEAN
were merged.

The enlarged arena of regional organization increased the
potential difficulties not only by the arithmetic addition of two
new states but also by a summation of the various difficulties
within the states as well. Indonesia, with its tremendous size
and diversity and its complex and contentious political life,
may be subject to at least as much conflict as the three original
ASA states. At the same time, the concentration in Singapore
of urban Chinese who could not be assimilated in the Federation of Malaysia is a challenge to the effectiveness of ASEAN
or any other Southeast Asian regional arrangement. The
United Kingdom is withdrawing its defensive presence from
Singapore, and this will modify the security situation and
make a large hole in Singapore's economy. Thus, it is clear
that ASEAN faces problems vastly more complex and intrac-
table than those that ASA survived.

The government of Thailand has also joined in several
arrangements, other than SEATO, that extend outside of
Southeast Asia. The most notable of these is the Asian and

Pacific Council (ASPAC), but there are other economic and specialized institutions such as the Asian Development Bank (ADB), the Southeast Asian Ministers of Education Secretariat (SEAMES), and the Mekong River Development Project.

With this experience, it is to be expected that the government of Thailand would develop a policy on regionalism. Behind Thailand's active policy in the region, we can see an intention to be heard in world councils. The Kingdom's leaders, besides seeking stability, are sensitive to the danger that their interests might be sacrificed to those of larger powers. The policy of dependence on the United States increases that danger. For Thailand, the best protection against the danger of over-dependence on the United States lies in the development of ties of mutual dependence linking states in the region whose interests are similar to those of Thailand and whose position in regard to outside powers is weaker than that of Bangkok. The Ministry of Foreign Affairs expressed this view at the time of the establishment of ASA:

> Closer cooperation among the countries of this region in the form of regional grouping is . . . of vital importance. It is a question of bare survival for these nations, because it will not be possible for them to compete with economically advanced countries on an equal footing so long as they do not unite with a view to restoring some sort of balance of power.*

Expressed in 1961, these rudimentary ideas have evolved into a doctrine of regionalism that is strikingly realistic in its assessment of potentialities. The doctrine contains two elements, both of which have been repeated frequently by the Foreign Minister of Thailand, Thanat Khoman.

The first element is national strength: "Each and every nation in Southeast Asia should do their utmost to consolidate

* Thailand, Ministry of Foreign Affairs, *Foreign Affairs Bulletin,* August-September, 1961, p. 34.

and promote their own national strength, their political structure, their economy, their human and material resouces. They should do so individually, and they can do better by working together in joint endeavours through regional and subregional cooperation."*

The second element is an ingenious solution to the simple fact that the military capacity of the Southeast Asian nations is small and poorly based. This element is

> . . . that regional security can best be maintained through close cooperation among Asian Countries forming a kind of "collective political defense." The term "political" is used here in its widest sense to encompass cooperation in economic, social and cultural fields as well, leaving outside of the scope the military activities. . . . Such a grouping will also serve to strengthen the hands of its member countries in dealing more adequately with external powers and will reduce the likelihood of outside interference.†

Such statements are unequivocal expressions of the aspiration of the leaders of Thailand to greater autonomy within a dismally oppressive world and of a realistic recognition on their part that any further enlargement of autonomy depends upon cooperative stability within the region. The Thai leaders know, on the basis of their own experience, that power is generated by settled cooperation within a state and among states. Consequently, they seek to encourage, by their participation, the growth of cooperation and the diminution of conflict in Southeast Asia.

* Thanat Khoman, "Building a Free Southeast Asia" (address delivered at the University of Minnesota), *Press Release No. 62* (New York: Permanent Mission of Thailand to the United Nations, October 22, 1968).

† Thanat Khoman, "Answers to Questions Posed by Yomuri Shimbun," *Press Release No. 42* (New York: Permanent Mission of Thailand to the United Nations, June 23, 1969).

IV

Security and National Integration

Security for the Kingdom of Thailand depends not only on external policy but also on internal conditions. The line between foreign, or external, policy and domestic, or internal, policy is frequently hard to establish. The open character of the economy links foreign trade and economic relations very closely to the domestic economy. At the same time, because of the turbulence of political affairs in the countries near Thailand (not only in Vietnam but also in Laos, Cambodia, Burma, and Malaysia) and because of the relatively unmobilized character of much of Thai society, security in the international world is linked closely to domestic peace.

The character and trends of national integration are, thus, closely related to national security. Policies aimed at enhancing integration are stimulated by the government's anticipation of possible disruptive or even revolutionary activities by internal political forces.

Among these forces are several that have subversive potentialities. Internal revolt is a threat to the Kingdom's integrity. Rebels and revolutionaries, in this day, often are closely associated with external powers. The Chinese Communist Government has frequently condemned the leaders of Thailand to the dust heap of history. Since 1954, China has been the residence of implicitly or explicitly rebellious Thai people who have been provided with facilities to pursue their ends. Since 1964, a front organization, or putative organization—the National Patriotic Front of Thailand—has been publicized by

Chinese media. (See Chapter V.) Rebellion is an authentically Thai style of politics. Therefore, the Thai Government has been adequately impressed by such a threat.

Effective and just national integration is the appropriate defense against this threat. Every society is divided into groups or categories of people that are related to each other by various institutions. In Thailand, two kinds of divisions have political significance: ethnic divisions and divisions between city and country.

Ethnic homogeneity is one of Thailand's great social strengths because 85–90 per cent of the population (which is estimated at between 33 million and 34 million) consists of Thai-speaking people pursuing a substantially similar way of life. Even so, ethnic and dialect-group differences are bases for some concern.

We may consider the Kingdom's population as divided into non-Thai and Thai linguistic groups. The non-Thai are divided into indigenous and immigrant groups, while the Thai people are divided into dialect groups. All of these groups have subcategories. Together, they are the building blocks of national integration, although the lines of distinction among them may lead to conflict.

From the American point of view, the most striking characteristic of these ethnic categories is their fluidity. Americans are inclined to think of ethnic characteristics as rather fixed, particularly when they are associated with different racial characteristics. This attitude prevails in the face of both the fact of assimilation and the idea of the "melting pot." Perhaps this is because one of the most important ethnic groups in the United States is the black people.

But ethnic difference in Thailand is not associated with physical characteristics. (In fact, physical characteristics are to some extent associated with social class in the minds of the Thai.) Instead, ethnicity is associated with the manner in which people behave, particularly their language or dialect.

In many cases, the ethnic difference of a group is largely a matter of agreement, regardless of behavior. This is also true of the Chinese minority in Thailand, whose situation there is more like that of European immigrants to the United States than like that of the Negroes in America. Thus, it is reasonable to investigate the point of view that ethnic differences are associated with more or less voluntary ways of behaving.

Perhaps half of the 90 per cent of the population of Thailand that is Thai is made up of ethnic groups of outlying regions—northerners, northeasterners, or southerners. Each of these groups has a more or less common dialect, and, within each, there is a more or less common sense of ethnic identity. But, within each, there are also many subgroups distinguished by dialect and custom, so it is appropriate to think of layers of identification or even situations of identification. It seems to be true that ethnic differences are used by people to define where they stand in regard to other groups for purposes of either cooperation or competition. Thus, a person is a *Phu Thai* in regard to other people in northeastern Thailand, a northeastern Thai in regard to the people of central Thailand, and a Thai in regard to the Chinese. Moreover, he can learn to speak various dialects of Thai and, thereby, become able to move around ethnically and be a *Phu Thai* at home and a central Thai in Bangkok or in the south. Or he may be a *Phu Thai* at a religious festival of people from either the Thai or Lao side of the Mekong River but a central Thai at a diplomatic meeting with the Lao in Vientiane. In short, with opportunities to move educationally and economically, ethnic identification among Thai is substantially voluntary and often purposeful. To a lesser extent, the same is true of non-Thai people in Thailand. (See Table I.)

From this point of view, ethnic differences are voluntary in principle, although the opportunities for any individual to make choices among ethnic groups vary with the economic resources and cultural facilities available to him.

TABLE I
Minority Peoples

Group	Estimated Population[a]	Location
Indigenous		
Malay	670,000	South-Malaysian border
Hill tribes[b]		
Meo	53,031	North
Yao	16,119	North
Karen	123,380	Northwest-Burmese border
Lahu	15,994	North
Lisu	9,440	North
Akha	6,442	North
Cambodian (Khmer, Kui)	230,000	East, southeast
Mon	60,000	Central plain—west of Bangkok
Immigrant		
Chinese	2,600,000	Urban areas—especially central Thailand
Vietnamese	74,750[c]	Northeast; Bangkok

SOURCES:

[a] Unless otherwise specified, all figures are estimates and statistics in Peter Kunstadter, ed., *Southeast Asian Tribes, Minorities, and Nations* (Princeton, N.J.: Princeton University Press, 1967) vol. I, pp. 371–72, 397–98.

[b] *Report of the United Nations Survey Team on the Economic and Social Needs of the Opium-Producing Areas in Thailand,* pp. 8 and 56 (Bangkok, 1967).

[c] Peter A. Poole, "Thailand's Vietnamese Minority," *Asian Survey,* vol. VII, no. 12, p. 887 (December, 1967).

Indigenous non–Thai-speaking groups live, for the most part, in border areas and are, therefore, considered susceptible to external manipulation.

Malays

Four provinces on the southern border of the Kingdom have a predominantly Malay-speaking population. In these days of ethnic nationalism, these provinces are a potential source of difficulty between Thailand and Malaysia. The government of Malaysia has said that it has no ambitions toward these provinces. Such a profession is probably genuine because of the delicate balance of ethnic relations within Malaysia. The Thai Government has taken it as genuine and, for the time being, is not concerned about external support for a Malay rebellion in Thailand.

Hill Tribes

In the mountains on the western and northern borders with Burma and Laos, there are perhaps 225,000 members of various non-Thai ethnic groups. These people, many of whom live in remote areas and most of whom have ethnic connections in Burma, Laos, or even southwestern China, present difficult problems. There is often antagonism among these groups, as well as antagonism between them and the Thai. Moreover, two problems connected with the economy of the hill people are bases of conflict. In the first place, their technique of agriculture involves burning the forests—a practice that the government deplores. Secondly, their principal cash crop—opium—is illegal and, therefore, involves a complex pattern of illicit trade and attendant racketeering.

All these tensions and potentiality for mischief located on the sensitive frontier area cause the government considerable worry. The tensions have occasioned no small amount of shooting, and the government suspects that Lao and Chinese Communist organizations are involved.

Cambodians

Along the northern border with Cambodia, in three provinces of Thailand, live an uncertain number of ethnic Cambodians. In general, this minority appears satisfied to live peacefully in the Thai Kingdom, but both Cambodia and Thailand fear that this ethnic minority group will provide a milieu for subversion.

Chinese

The second type of non-Thai minority group is the immigrants. Chinese are by far the most numerous among immigrant minorities, although 50,000–80,000 Vietnamese live in the northeastern provinces. The overseas Chinese have been an issue in Thai politics since 1910. During those years, however, the issue has changed several times. The problem comes down to two questions: Who is a Chinese, and what is the nature of the distinction between the Thai and the Chinese? By some ethnic definitions, there may be as many as 3 million Chinese in Thailand. In order to reach this large figure, it is necessary to include many people who are Chinese by virtue of their descent. Traditionally, Chinese immigrants have been wage laborers and merchants. They have been thought to dominate Thailand's commercial activity by means of ethnic solidarity, which led to a position of commercial privilege. This economic domination was considered a political threat, again because of ethnic solidarity, as well as a tendency for the Chinese community to be actively interested in the politics of China. Thus, the Chinese have been considered a reservoir of political strength and personnel for China's pursuit of influence in Thailand. They have also been subject to the pressure of economic nationalism.

None of these worries may be considered unreasonable, although responses to them have been of varying degrees of effectiveness. Chinese business practices are based on insider-outsider distinctions, which are based on families and family-based institutions. The most important institution of this kind is the bank. Certainly, for many years, Chinese bankers operated in a way that was discriminatory to the non-Chinese, as well as to some Chinese. Chinese-dominated labor organizations have operated similarly.

At the same time, the politics of China has influenced Chinese living in Thailand. Since imperial times, Chinese political figures have raised money and sought support in Bangkok. The struggles of the Chinese civil wars, particularly between the Nationalist and Communist parties and governments, have been reflected in the Bangkok Chinese community. Young people have been recruited, schools and teachers have been involved, and control of local Chinese organizations has been at stake. These activities could not be insulated from Thai politics. Moreover, those policies of the Thai Government aimed specifically at Chinese have brought general response from this community. The most dramatic instance occurred immediately after the defeat of Japan, when a riot in Bangkok burst out in belated protest against the government's anti-Chinese policies before and during the war.

Since World War II, the Thai Government has developed a rather sophisticated policy toward the Chinese question. This policy basically encourages assimilation of Chinese into Thai society by combining efforts to limit political and economic activities based on ethnic differences between Chinese and Thai with a policy of removing obstacles that hinder the Chinese from becoming Thai.

The government's policy drastically limits new immigration; it disables aliens, but permits naturalization and disables, in certain ways, a member of the second generation, unless he gets a Thai education or serves in the government, *and, thus, acts like a Thai.* At the same time, the government has tried, with some success, to break the practice of discriminatory banking and discourage the intrusion of the politics of China into Chinese institutions in Thailand. Finally, in business, Chinese-Thai cooperation has become widespread and often successful.

The effect of these tendencies is to reward assimilation while still penalizing the persistence of Chinese culture and behavior. Social attitudes support this approach to the problem, both by disapproving being Chinese and accepting assimilation.

Vietnamese

The 40,000 to 50,000 Vietnamese in the towns of the northeastern provinces have been dealt with less successfully. These communities moved into the country as refugees from the wars in Vietnam, particularly in the 1940's. The people have maintained a community cohesion, as well as an interest in the affairs of Vietnam. Political struggles in Vietnam have influenced the organization among these communities, which for the most part have stayed aloof from their Thai neighbors, except in commercial matters.

The position of these communities is considered temporary by both sides, however unrealistic this attitude may be. The government has cooperated with both Vietnamese governments to assist in repatriating these people, and a large number did, in fact, return to their homes in North Vietnam between 1957 and 1965.

The Thai Government has been alarmed by the presence of these Vietnamese communities. Unlike that of the Chinese, their situation is neither of long standing nor governed by a well-developed notion of their position. The idea that these alien communities serve as a base for North Vietnamese operations that are hostile to Thailand is by no means fantastic. The political interest of these people, insofar as they have one, is certainly oriented toward Vietnam. Their community organizations are under the influence, if not the control, of organizations in North Vietnam, the original home of most of the people. The people's loyalty to Ho Chi Minh was expressed quietly but openly. These community organizations are effective and present the Thai with a difficult problem of control. For example, the repatriation was carried out with the cooperation of these organizations, no doubt with the effect of strengthening their hold over their people.

From time to time, the government has threatened to move all Vietnamese out of the northeastern region, and, in 1953,

1,500 were, in fact, transported. But there is great reluctance to carry out such massive resettlement, in view of the political and economic problems it would entail. In any case, the threat remains as an implement of control.

Dialect Groups

Among the 90 per cent of the population who speak the Thai language, there are also many ethnic distinctions. The Thai-Lao of the provinces of northeastern Thailand, in the bend of the Mekong between Thailand and Laos, have been the most alarming because of real or imagined schemes, supported from abroad, for separating provinces of the northeast from the Kingdom. I will return to the issues of the northeast in a later chapter, but the matter has been part of the subversion problem. There are dialect groups with considerable self-conscious differences from the dominant central Thai in both the north and the southern peninsula.

Since the 1890's, all Thai government's policies have been framed on the assumption of national uniformity. Under pressure from the imperialists, the government was impelled to reduce the diversity and potential divisions within the country in its quest for a national society. Therefore, administration, education, legal status, and all other such matters were approached on a national basis. Not until 1933 was local self-government introduced, and, even then, it was a uniform national scheme. Local problems and differences were treated as administrative details.

Such an approach was perfectly reasonable under the circumstances of external pressure and generally rather thin governmental programs. Particularly after the French and British had stabilized the border situation so that the threat of splitting parts of the country away diminished, a deliberate attempt to consolidate the internal society in a uniform way was progressive and effective.

In recent years, the unstable, even revolutionary, external situation, troubled by ethnic problems in Burma, Malaya, and Indochina, together with a much more active internal policy of development and social change, has stimulated challenges to the policy of uniformity. Regional and ethnic demands for special solutions are a part of the political life of the country.

The manner of responding to them, however, is a major issue. Several alternatives have seen light. The government is trying to devise means for more local administrative autonomy through decentralization. It has also set up regional development committees, drawn up regional development plans, and set up a committee for dealing with hill-tribe problems and an office concerned with hill-tribe welfare. Regional universities have been established. Efforts to vitalize local self-government are under way. All of these activities run against the strong and reasonable tradition of uniformity that has been implemented through administrative centralization. The outcome of this complicated effort is not at all clear.

Physical Differences

The Thai, being wet-rice farmers, live in river valleys and alluvial plains and floodplains where there is adequate water for rice cultivation. But there are differences in the different parts of the country. In the central part is the floodplain delta of the Chao Phraya River and several small rivers flowing into the Gulf of Siam. The land is extensive, flat, and fertile. Monsoon rains and annual floods virtually ensure enough water and natural fertilizer to grow millions of tons of rice every year. The principal kingdom of the Thai has been in this region for 500 years, moving from Sukothai, at the northern rim, to Ayudhaya and, finally, Bangkok, nearer the river mouth. Thus, the environment, by providing reliable conditions for supporting a large population and producing an agricultural surplus, furnishes a basis for urban life and political sophistication.

The geography of the north is characterized by small rivers and alluvial plains separated by high, forested mountains. Soils and water in these valleys also are suitable for rice cultivation, and the techniques of water control in a mountainous environment are such that small-scale cooperation can regulate water for flooding and irrigation. Here, the Thai have developed a more intensive pattern of agriculture capable of supporting a dense population in the valleys. Non-Thai people—Karen, Lisu, Akha, Lahu, Yao, and Meo—have learned to cultivate the mountainside with a technology that is also being adopted by Thai under pressure of population. By this means, both rice and other crops, of which the most notorius is opium, are produced.

In the northeast, the natural environment is less favorable to rice than in either the center or the north. Neither rainfall, flooding, nor soil is particularly well suited to rice cultivation, and the reliability of crops is, therefore, much lower than in the other regions. Nevertheless, 10 million Thai live in this area and do the best they can. The people of the northeast also produce animals for both draft and food, as well as a variety of crops that are not so dependent upon water supply. On low mountains and hills in the northeast are vast areas of forests that are sparsely populated and meagerly productive. The northeastern region produces barely enough to support its own population.

The character of the south is largely determined by the fact that it is a narrow and mountainous peninsula. Short, rapid rivers run both east and west into the sea, and people congregate on tiny floodplains to grow rice. In the extreme south, the heavy rain and true tropical climate provide conditions suitable for rubber cultivation, and many smallholders manage groves that they tap for shipment to the international market. Tin-mining is also an important activity that helps support the nonfarming population. For these reasons, the character of the south is less completely that of a rice-growing people, even though the Thai of the region still predominantly follow that occupation.

Thus, each region's environment has forced differences of social and economic situation on the peoples living there. Still, the imperatives of rice cultivation, particularly dependence on floodwater rather than rainfall, have produced the fundamental pattern of settlement of the country. People live in river valleys, not in rolling country, and, therefore, the distribution of population within the regions is very uneven.

Differences of Investment and Services

Historically, investment and government services have not been uniformly distributed throughout the country. If we again exclude the rubber-growing and mining south, which has participated in the Malayan pattern, it is clear that central Thailand was the area of heaviest investment and services for many years. The economic development of the Chao Phraya delta region has been substantial in the decades since 1870. This growth can be attributed principally to investment in canals for drainage, irrigation, and transportation, and to the port of Bangkok—and, secondarily, to better educational and health services in this region. In contrast, the northeastern region, with its vast distances and difficult terrain, was neglected until recently. Although railroads reached into the region in the 1920's, it was not until twenty years after World War II that the first genuine highway connecting the northeast with Bangkok was built. The same situation applies to investment in water control and power sources, as well as to government services. Between these extremes, the northern part of the country, for a variety of reasons, has found a middle way.

By restricting access to markets and limiting the possible

use of new technology, this difference of investment in the outlying regions has affected the rate of growth and the penetration of the outside world. For these reasons, the level of development of different regions of Thailand is quite varied.

Social Class and the Community

Wide difference of social class is another potential dimension of disintegration in Thailand. A person's social class is determined largely by how wealthy and educated he is, not directly by his family background. In other words, class is not hereditary. But the opportunity anyone has to study at a university or even a high school, not to mention gaining substantial wealth, is affected by the position of his family. Sons of the rich tend to be rich; sons of the educated tend to be educated. Even though "equal opportunity" is a principle of the Thai society, opportunity turns out not to be so equal in practice. Such a paradox is not unfamiliar to Americans.

In Thailand, however, the number of young people who have a chance to go through high schools and universities is small. The main limitation is that there are relatively few schools, and these are located in towns or cities. The only school available for the children of small-holding farmers is probably a one-room school with four classes and one teacher. Such a school will probably not prepare the child to enter a higher school, even if his family could afford to send him to town. Thus, the unmobilized society of Thailand displays an uneven distribution of the means to acquire education and advance to a career different from that of the previous generation.

More than the actual distribution of wealth and education, however, it is the difference of living style that attenuates the integration of social classes in Thailand. The great bulk of the population, living in a style dictated by small-hold peasant agriculture, may not be without wealth or culture. Such people usually own some valuable land and follow a civilized, if somewhat archaic and laborious, way of life. But their main concerns are very different from the concerns of the townsmen, particularly of the educated ones. The major concerns of the farmers are religion and agriculture, while those of the townsmen are social status and money.

Every country has within it divisions that, under some circumstances, could bring disintegration. In this respect, Thailand is no worse than any other place. In fact, it is much better off than many of its neighbors because it has many workable institutions that hold things together. Moreover, the government is pursuing policies that have, as their principal objective, better integration. The issue facing Thailand is whether or not the institutions will continue to serve as bridges between different parts of the community during a time of profound change when there are people who would seize upon the differences as a base from which to disintegrate and revolutionize the community in a radical and violent manner.

The Buddhist institutions, the government, the schools, and the system of commerce and industry permeate all of Thailand and work to hold disparate parts of the country together. The government is an administrative machine that operates through 71 provinces, about 500 districts, about 5,000 communes (administrative groupings of villages), and about 40,000 villages to provide, in at least a minimal way, civil order, social services (health, agricultural extension), and administration of facilities (roads, irrigation works, communications systems) throughout the country. Professional civil servants man the organizations of the central government down to the district level, while, in the rural areas, local part-time officials serve in the villages. Some 120 towns and markets are self-governing municipalities that are closely supervised by the central government.

This machinery, although widespread and manned by competent people, is, in fact, rather tenuous in many parts of the country. Rural areas, for the most part, rely on informal self-government to solve such public problems as they have. When they are faced with problems beyond their capacity, such as protection against bandits or other marauders, or construction of capital works such as roads or schools, villages must turn to the government, whose resources and manpower are relatively inadequate. At the same time, the government, on its own initiative, is attempting to construct works, extend technology, and provide protection—all of which require more money and trained men than are available. In short, the government's ability to cope with the strains of a changing society—strains that are sometimes increased by its own efforts—is stretched thin. Observers are alarmed by the gap between social demands and the government's capacity to meet them. The significance of this gap is obvious, in terms of maintaining authority and order when they are challenged by revolutionaries. It is feared that a revolutionary movement organized by Communists and supported from Laos, North Vietnam, and China could penetrate this gap to create a rural insurrection and, in the end, could march on Bangkok and seize power.

Integrating Institutions

Before considering the likelihood of this possibility, it will be worthwhile to enrich the picture by looking at the institutions, other than the government, that hold the country together. Buddhism is the professed and practiced religion of most Thai. It is so widespread that part of the definition of a Thai is his Buddhism, even though some Thai are Christians or Muslims. Buddhism is organized in temples or monasteries where monks live and practice the appropriate rituals. Almost every village community of the country supports—both morally and economically—a Buddhist monastery. It is customary for every man to spend a period of his life as a monk, usually in his community monastery. The Thai believe in their religion and treat it with an unselfconscious seriousness that is almost medieval.

The monasteries and, thus, the monks are ruled by a religious government that parallels, in most respects, the national government. This institution provides for the orderly practice of religion and thereby contributes to national integration. People can move throughout the country and find cordial hospitality in the monasteries. The hierarchy of church organization serves to formalize, regularize, and nationalize the social leadership and authority of monks.

The educational system also penetrates throughout the land and serves to link the regions and classes. The school system, in part, emerged from the monasteries, which, in former times, provided some education to the children of the villages. Today, the school system is similar to the religious institutions, although less effective in maintaining its grip on the people. Thailand has had compulsory elementary education since 1921, and today there are 23,000 elementary schools, which teach more than 3 million children. For all practical purposes, every child in the Kingdom can reach a school. The teachers are employed by the government, and the curriculum is established by the Ministry of Education.

This system is not without its defects. The curriculum was designed to "nationalize" the children and is not completely appropriate to their needs, not to mention their desires. An aspect of this "nationalizing" can be noted in the fact that teaching is carried on in the central Thai dialect, which is often difficult for, if not offensive to, regional groups. Good reasons stand behind this approach, however, and the schools unquestionably extend the understanding of people in general about Thailand as a nation. The poor quality, ineffective methods, and poverty of materials are more serious defects. Teachers are inadequately trained, and paper, books, pencils, and, even, buildings are in short supply. All these defects combine to make school something less than it might be for the country children.

The ultimate defect lies in the difficulty of continuing beyond the first four years. Compulsory education was extended from four to seven years recently, but the schools and teachers for grades five through seven are still not available in many places. Beyond seventh grade, high schools are even fewer and more expensive to attend, so that country schools, at the present time, do not give most farm children much chance to improve their position in society. Therefore, this incentive does not infuse the educational system with the energy for social improvement.

The government has not settled on an approach to this problem, for plausible reasons. A difficulty that is common to many places in the world is the problem of the unemployed intellectual. Many countries have educated people who are difficult to absorb into the economy because their education is not appropriate. They are usually overeducated in a clerical or literary way and either unwilling or unable to take up the laborious jobs that need filling. This kind of a population is often turbulent and vociferously dissident. Thailand has not had this difficulty, largely because of restrictions on higher education.

At present, the expanding Thai economy requires more and more educated or trained people, so enlargement of the school system is timely. Nevertheless, disputes go on as to the appropriate way to enlarge the system—whether through vocational or academic schools—as well as disputes over whether, for example, to emphasize enlargement or improvement. Limitations of money to pay for new facilities make such disputes lively if not bitter.

In sum, the school system does link the country, however imperfectly. The dialect of central Thailand has become the national language, and the image of the Thai nation is widely recognized. The schools offer some limited opportunity for young people to move themselves into new and better careers. This framework, which is at present inadequate, is in place and can be used to enlarge and improve the educational opportunities for more and more people.

Business is the third major institution that bridges some of the gaps in the Thai community. Within Thailand, there is much movement of merchandise. Commercial crops are collected, and manufactured goods are distributed. And some of the commercial crops such as rice, tobacco, kenaf, cotton, and tapioca require some milling or manufacturing. People looking for work also move around the country in response to opportunities in mills, construction sites, and factories. All of this movement of goods and people depends on transportation and on a system of markets, middlemen, and money.

In the past decade, the government has built or improved roads all over the country. Buses and trucks seem to follow the bulldozers into the rural areas, carrying goods and buyers in and bringing goods, customers, and workers out. The amount of productive effort that follows a road is extraordinary.

The key to this activity seems to be the capacity of commercial enterprise to make a market in commodities. This may be as simple as merely offering cash for a crop that can be grown on hillside land but usually involves a complicated combination of technical assistance and credit. Farmers need seeds, fertilizer, and insecticides, as well as knowledge that there is a market. The commercial traders or processors looking for the crop are required to provide these things as well as buy the produce. Standing behind the middlemen are bankers, who have extended bank branches to every province of the Kingdom.

The capacity of the system to penetrate the country is striking, although the quality and stability of the penetration are imperfect. Credit arrangements are difficult, money is in short supply and inflated, prices fluctuate, often wildly, and contracts do not always work. The level of organization of markets in different commodities varies from the highly developed system for the production of Virginia tobacco to the chaos of the jute market. In all cases, the tendency is toward a more organized effort to stabilize the market.

The tendency toward organization is perhaps the most serious threat to economic activity, because of the intervention of political power. In some commodities—notoriously, hogs for the Bangkok and export markets—regulatory monoplies supported by political powers have managed to decrease production and participation in the market by driving down prices to the farmer. Activities of a similar kind have been seen in other crops. An alternative approach to the organization problem—one that should lead to more beneficial results—is to dominate the market with heavy use of such services as credit and quality-control. Efforts toward this end, for example, in the feed-corn market, have so far enjoyed dubious success.

Despite all these imperfections, the commercial enterprises display striking energy in their capacity to penetrate the country and develop productive and mutually beneficial relationships with farmers.* Commerce acts to link different social groups of the country, and the responsiveness of different groups to economic opportunities demonstrates the vitality of the system. The potential of this kind of linkage to bridge social gaps appears to be great. But the new linkages are also new opportunities for unproductive and exploitative economic relations and, thus, are fraught with peril.

None of these linking institutions could work without the towns and small cities of the country. Despite the fact that 75 per cent of the population is agricultural, Thai society is based on a town culture. There is a word in the Thai language, *myang,* which can be variously translated as city, town,

---

* See T. H. Silcock, ed., *Thailand: Social and Economic Studies in Development* (Durham, N.C.: Duke University Press, 1967).

country, state, world, province, and perhaps other ways. It is a very commonly used word. If it has a general meaning, it is this: a place where people live that has a town as its core. From this term, we can see that the basic Thai notion of a community seems to be a town or city with its surrounding, interdependent countryside.

The town is the seat of power and civilization—the location of governmental, religious, cultural, and economic institutions. In contemporary Thailand, the cities and towns serve just this purpose. There are perhaps 150 to 200 such centers of various sizes, with populations ranging from 10,000 to 100,000 people. Bangkok is, of course, the great city, with a population of about 2 million. Altogether, there are 120 incorporated self-governing cities and another 500 semi-autonomous "sanitary districts" of varying degrees of urban character.

Government offices, large monasteries, high schools, markets, branch banks, and links in the networks of transportation and communication are located in towns. The societies of these towns include a number of people—government officials, monks, teachers, and businessmen—who are actively involved in national institutions and participate in national affairs. Most of these institutions have main offices in Bangkok, although their immediate affairs may be subordinate to a large town or provincial center. At the same time, there are people in almost every agricultural community who have regular contact with the central town. These rural people may be village headmen, monastery abbots, schoolteachers, or commercial farmers. There are also people, such as buyers, salesmen, and transportation workers, whose work connects the towns with the villages.

Thailand is not an expanse of completely self-contained villages. On the contrary, the life of the villages and that of the towns are interdependent, not only economically but also, less tangibly, in terms of information, authority, and consolation.

The importance of these links and their configuration, both in active institutions and physical locations and movements, is difficult to overestimate. Thai society, seen as consisting of the governmental upper class in Bangkok, which rules the mass of unconnected, self-contained, and more or less sullen villages, presents a picture entertained and perpetuated by more than one observer. There is sufficient truth in this picture, particularly if one observes only the activities and officials of the government, to make it plausible and even persuasive. Rural Thailand is unmobilized and, in many places, isolated from the mainstream of national life. Government services are often practically nonexistent, and the effectiveness of schools, religious connections, and the market attenuates in many places. Nevertheless, the relations between Bangkok and the villages, by way of cities and towns, are much more active than is commonly thought.

The existence of these relations in the form of institutions provides a basis for modifying the relations and expanding the flow of goods and services. Such a process can be developed without abrupt change in the institutional order, although, taken together, the potential changes might well constitute a revolution.

It is this vision of change which raises the problem of whether Thailand can remain stable while meeting the imperatives of the contemporary world. Is it possible to mobilize the people and resources of Thailand to attain a more productive economy while continuing to provide justice and preserve freedom? Or will the framework collapse under the strain of new requirements? Finally, will the strains provide an opportunity for foreign-supported revolutionaries to mobilize and organize the people to destroy the existing system in Thailand and replace it with another, Maoist, one?

V

Communism and Insurrection

It is difficult to write about rural insurrection in Thailand, because there has not been very much of it. Peasant revolts have played very little part in the history of the Thai, and the present troubles are quite restricted. The question has assumed some importance because of the declared intention of the Chinese Communists to use the technique of "revolutionary war," based on peasant insurrection, to extend their influence. The Chinese declaration resounds in the echo chamber of anxiety created by Vietnam and becomes that much more impressive. At the same time, some observers think that the changes taking place in Thailand are undermining the stability of social and political relations and bringing about conditions conducive to insurrection. There is little evidence, however, to guide us through this maze of speculation.

At the present time, there are perhaps several thousand people in a state of insurrection in remote parts of Thailand. Three areas—the Phu Phan Mountains in the Northeast, the mountains of Chiangrai, Nan, and Petchabun provinces in the North, and the heavy forests of the Malaya border area—provide shelter for different groups. The history and position of each of these groups are different so that it is difficult to determine whether they are connected in any organized way.

Northeastern Thailand

The Phu Phan Mountains are a chain of heavily forested and thinly populated hills that form an arc parallel to the great curve of the Mekong River. The northern and eastern slopes run down into the river valley. The ridge separates Mekong Laos from the central provinces of northeast Thailand drained by the Mun and Chi rivers.

The Thai, including the Thai-Lao of northeast Thailand, are a riverine people whose civilization is focused on river towns and whose economy is based on irrigated rice-cultivation. Thus, the mountains of Phu Phan are something of a no man's land, unfit for settled people. Their remoteness is cultural, since Thai people find no comfort in hills or forests. This remoteness makes the mountains a refuge from authority and a sanctuary for outlaws. Bandits and cattle rustlers have always hidden themselves away here. Since at various points the mountains come near the river, which is the border with Laos, this sanctuary has also served smugglers between the two countries. This pattern has served the purposes of insurgents as well.

Small bands of armed men can hide indefinitely in the remote terrain, sallying forth to intimidate or persuade villages that are located near the mountains. Food is obtainable by these means, and perhaps young men can be impressed or recruited for service. The length of the range from south to north is about 150 miles and from east to west about 100 miles. The sanctuary touches on a wide area of the country. Moreover, the smugglers' routes serve to link the mountain area with Laos and, ultimately, North Vietnam and China. Altogether the Phu Phan Mountains provide an excellent situation for mounting the rudiments of an insurrection against the government.

Conditions have been politically and administratively good for insurgents. This northeastern part of northeast Thailand is the most remote area of the country. Transportation was, until recently, limited to poor roads and the river. The authority and activities of the distant central government have been at a minimum. Culture centers and towns that focus the civilization are as often in Laos as in Thailand. A tradition of resistance to central Thai influence is long and strong, and local political leaders have sustained their positions by dissent from Bangkok's bidding. The people of the area have become deeply attached to their leaders in an emotional, almost religious, fashion, which reflects an important contrast between this part of Thailand and the rest. Here, the old patterns of social relations were less infused with Indian and Cambodian notions of the "god-king" and more approximate to the idea of the lord as a "father of the people." There is among these Lao an old idea of a folk leader who is infused with a "good spirit" and who might arise for the benefit of all.

The least attractive side of the situation in this area of the northeast is that several of the most renowned leaders have been killed for political reasons in Bangkok. Four members of parliament from the northeast were murdered in 1949, and another member was murdered in 1952. The murders were apparently carried out by the police for political reasons, mainly because these men were leaders of the then dying but still important Free Thai movement and were associated with the exiled former Prime Minister Pridi Phanomyong.*

In 1961, another member of parliament from the area, Krong Chandawong, was executed by authority of the Prime Minister's emergency powers. Krong was adjudged to be the local leader of a Chinese Communist–supported clandestine organization in this area.

Regardless of the legal status of these deaths, and a legal execution is rather different from a police murder, the effect on the people of the area was strong. They were confirmed in their attitude of opposition to Bangkok and their assumption of discriminatory treatment against the Thai-Lao in Thailand.

In all of these cases, it has been said that the leadership of

* The Free Thai movement was an organization developed during World War II to implement resistance to Japan in Thailand. It received support from American and British sources. Pridi Phanomyong was the leading Thai figure at the time. After the war, it became a political organization of younger people who supported the governments of Pridi and his colleague Luang Thamrong Nawasawat in 1946 and 1947. Many of the leaders of the Free Thai movement were from northeastern Thailand.

the remote northeast seeks to separate these provinces from the country and, presumably, join Laos as an independent state. Whether such a notion has ever been seriously entertained by anybody is problematical. The advantages of being part of Thailand compared with being part of Laos are clear to the most obtuse. Nevertheless, the utility of such an argument when used to pry more resources and greater responsiveness from Bangkok is also not difficult to see.

In any case, the combination of remoteness, economic isolation, government indifference, and cultural and political dissent serves as a plausible, and perhaps fertile, ground for insurrection. The degree to which it has taken hold is less impressive. Since 1964, small bands, whose estimated total size has ranged from a few hundred to 3,000 men, have operated in these mountains. Raids, terrorism, and more or less forced propaganda meetings have been thrust into the villages at the foot of the mountains. Apparently, some villages came under the regular influence of the movement. An indeterminate number of organizers have found a place in a greater number of villages. The rate of incidents—shootings, food raids, or meetings—ranged all along the mountains and increased between 1964 and 1967. Thereafter, incidents and estimates of the number of armed terrorists declined.

The effect of this on the government has been considerable, and a range of methods has been developed to cope with the situation. They include protective measures—more police protection, recruitment of local defense forces, military sweeps and patrols, more communications—and schemes for development and service—road building, community development, well digging. These activities of the government, supported by assignment of civil and military officials of good quality, appear to have ended the growth of the insurgent organization and operations. Long-range plans for regional development at an accelerated pace may provide the basis for liquidating it completely.

Northern Thailand

The second area of active insurrection is in Petchabun, Nan, and southeastern Chiangrai provinces, a region of high, forested mountains. In this area, the border between Thailand and Laos is not the river, but the watershed. These mountains are the bailiwick of the aggressive and mobile Meo people, who seem to be at the bottom of the trouble.

The Meo live high up in the mountains of southern China, northern Laos, and northern Thailand. They live in something like a tribal organization and exploit the high mountain slopes by burning off the forests and cultivating the clearings, until the land is exhausted. Then, the tribes move on to new areas. For hundreds of years, they appear to have been moving southward, looking for new forest sites and escaping from the pressure of lowland peoples—Chinese, Lao, Thai, and others. The Meo are devoted to their way of life, fiercely independent, and aggressively combative toward other people. They are the principal cultivators of the opium poppy and know well the use of firearms.

In defense of their position, the Meo have sought and made alliances and played the politics of the lowlands. Pragmatists, they are indifferent to such issues as Communism and care only about opium markets and land. There is no Meo nation and, in Laos, Meo groups are to be found on both sides of the Lao sector of the Indochina war.

In northern Thailand, the Meo have been extending their area of operation since their first appearance fifty to seventy-five years ago. The settled people view them as intruders and fear them, because the Meo are destructive and aggressive, and because they spread opium addiction. Because other non-Thai people—Karen and Yao, for example—are usually settled between the Meo and the Thai, the possibility of Meo deals with Thai officials, deals at the expense of others, have not escaped the Meo. Nevertheless, the Thai Government is, in general, unsympathetic to Meo behavior.

The complications of ethnic, ideological, and opium issues make this situation almost impossible to sort out. For fifteen years, the Thai Government has been trying to develop a consistent policy toward the question of "hill tribes," that is, all non-Thai people living in the mountains. So far, there is no stable policy. The issues involve many interests and points of view and cut across a number of agencies. At the same time, several less than consistent programs have been put in operation. In short the situation in the hills is very confused.

In 1967, hostilities broke out between the Thai police and a group of Meo, and a village was burned down. Whether this had to do with opium or some similar matter is not clear, but those events escalated the fighting. The Meo operations, based on the Lao side of the border, show sophistication in tactics and weapons. The army took over command and adopted a "strategy" of warning people in the hills to leave and then assuming any who remained were hostile. A certain amount of napalm and high explosives has been used on hill villages with rather total results. The trouble with this approach is obvious: It is only crudely discriminatory and tends to enlarge the area of hostilities. In 1969, after some dramatic failures, the army returned operations against these insurgents to civil leadership. An effort is now under way to develop small units of Meo men to assist in the suppression of rebel activity. A greater degree of success may be anticipated. In any case, the small war of the Thai against the Meo, now in its third year, has become involved in the ideological struggle with the Communists. On both the Communist and Thai sides, the Meo are identified as Communist-dominated insurgents associated, through Laos, with Hanoi and Peking.

Southern Thailand

The third area of difficulty is in the extreme south on the border with Malaysia. From a time early in the Malayan

Emergency of 1948–58, the Communist anti-government forces, which were and are Malayan Chinese, found some sanctuary in the forests of the Thai-Malay border. After the Emergency ended, a few continued to maintain themselves there.

The Thai police were tolerant because they considered this group to be oriented toward Malaya (since 1963, called Malaysia) and to be no threat to Thailand. It is not impossible that some bribery was involved in this tolerant attitude, but it is probably true that the objectives of the group, which calls itself the Malayan Races' Liberation Army (MRLA), lie in Malaysia.

The area along the southern border is distinctive, like the areas of the far northeast and the northern mountains. The population is predominantly Malay-speaking Muslim people indigenous to these forests. There is also a conspicuous Chinese minority community, involved in tin mining and the rubber trade. The center of the Chinese population is the rail-junction town of Hadyai, thirty miles from the Malaysian border. Thus, in ethnic as well as economic terms, this part of Thailand is very similar to Malaysia. Given tolerance from the Thai Government, the MRLA could operate here just as they had on the other side of the border.

The situation is delicate, however, because the Malay population has, from time to time, been restive under central government policies. Because of the strong pull of Chinese in Malaysia, the Chinese in the south are also less well integrated into Thai society than is the case with Chinese in the rest of the country.

In 1964, the situation was complicated by the surreptitious intervention of Indonesia as part of that country's since aborted "confrontation" with Malaysia. Indonesian money and, perhaps, people sought to arouse some enthusiasm among the local Malays for a greater Malaya under Indonesian leadership. The degree to which this activity was coordinated with the Communist Chinese MRLA is difficult to estimate.

In any case, the Thai Government came to the conclusion that a greater effort to control the area was warranted.

For years, during the Emergency and after, the Government of Malaysia tried to develop a joint Thai-Malay operation to suppress the MRLA. The Thai Government did very little beyond talking about such an operation, however, until 1965. In that year, an agreement was reached to establish two centers for joint operations in southern Thailand, and some troops were moved into the area. In the succeeding years, there have been a number of armed clashes, and several MRLA bases have been raided. The thick forests and poor communications make the effort to capture these small, well-organized and entrenched forces very difficult. They have had years to establish their position and develop a system of support that extends into the Chinese population of the towns and cities. Nevertheless, their ethnic distinction as Chinese is a limiting weakness as well as a strength. With determination, the Thai and Malays should be able to contain the Malayan Chinese in their present confined position.

The challenge of these insurrections is that they may be transformed from isolated ethnic uprisings into a revolutionary movement capable of overturning the political and social structure of Thailand and substituting a style of politics and social organization peculiar to the Communist world. To assess the possibility of this, some understanding is required of the historical role of force in Thailand's politics, as well as of the character and potential of revolutionary war.

Force in Politics

In spite of the fact that peasant insurrection has not been important in Thailand's history, force in politics has been common. Since the end of the absolute monarchy in 1932, conspiracy and *coup d'état* have, together, assumed a central position in political life. In the years since then, there have been at least ten suppressed conspiracies or actual *coups d'état*. These events have given Thailand a reputation for a political life based on force and violence, a reputation that is deserved but often misunderstood.

A more or less secret conspiratorial *coup d'état* based on military control has become the established way to change the government. This kind of event can most properly be understood as analogous to an election in the United States. At the same time, it is another symptom of invalid constitutionalism and unrepresentative government in the Kingdom.

Even after the ending of the absolute monarchy, political power has remained attached to the formal leaders of the military and civil bureaucracy. Since the system of elected parliaments has not been able to generate power adequate to control the government, let alone change the principal office-holders, it is not possible to remove a prime minister and cabinet within the framework of the constitution. Nevertheless, if for any one of various reasons, change of government becomes desirable to influential people and organizations, some means will be found and the means is the coup.

But the arena of such changes has been restricted to those people who hold high bureaucratic office. The conspiracies that formulate the coups may extend into the lower levels of the government organizations, and the cliques and bureaucratic factions based on loyalty, patronage, and favoritism have their role to play. But these organizations never penetrate the general public. The success of a *coup d'état* seems to depend upon a kind of public opinion that approves a change of government and supports the extension of the conspiracy but, other than in that way, *coups d'état* are inside jobs.

The degree of actual violence, if measured in casualty rates, of these coups has been small. Such a nonviolent kind of force is probably a result of the restricted arena of the affair, as well as the fairly well-established rules of winning and losing. Demonstrated control over certain organizations has usually been adequate to persuade one side that the other side has won. It is rather like resigning a game of chess. Thus, the basic character of the coup is a show of power, similar to an election victory. It is a show of power over the army usually and thus implies that behind the power is force and behind the force is violence.

As a consequence, Thailand's reputation for force and violence in politics has its own peculiarity, arising from the restricted character of Thai politics. Presumably, this peculiarly formal and nearly bloodless style depends upon the persistence of limited political interest and participation in the country; that is, this style depends upon the unmobilized economic, social, and political life. But because the government has embarked on an irreversible course of development, it is plausible to suspect that these conditions will not persist forever, nor even for very long.

Therefore, revolutionary war assumes a kind of plausibility. If we recognize a historical Thai willingness to accept forced political change, together with rapid changes in the economic and social structures of the country, we can see that a basis for revolution may be emerging. The possibility of success depends on the character of revolutionary war and the vulnerabilities of the situation.

Revolutionary War

The ideas of this kind of war, which Communist thinkers call "wars of national liberation," have been distilled principally from the experience of the Chinese revolution and the Vietnamese war against France, with some Algerian and Cuban evidence thrown into the pot. In brief, the experience is thought to demonstrate that a determined leadership can gradually mobilize a fighting force from among a peasant population. This primitive fighting force can operate according to guerrilla tactics—basically, hit, run, hide—against a superior force in such a way as to harass and harm it. At the same time, a political organization can be developed among lightly governed peasants by a combination of persuasion, based on promises to solve local problems, and coercion, based on the ability of the fighting force. The political organization and the fighting force, if they can be controlled by a cadre of Communist Party members, can be erected into a government and an army that drives out the existing government and replaces it. The new government is based on a peasantry mobilized by the process of the revolutionary war itself.

The sequence of Marxist ideas put forth to explain this process begins with the belief that the world is presently dominated by a titantic struggle between emerging socialism and doomed, but still vigorous, capitalist imperialism. Socialism's victory depends upon the certain, but not yet realized, alliance of the workers and peasants, which will be led by the Communist Party. This alliance will struggle against and, ultimately, defeat the non-Communist governments of the world, called in Communist rhetoric, "imperialism and its lackeys." The appropriate strategy for this struggle is for the underdeveloped nations of the world, the world's countryside, so to speak, to surround the industrial countries and defeat them. In order that this be possible, it is necessary to liberate the underdeveloped countries from imperialism, which works through its lackeys in the local governments, especially those governments allied with the United States. All those classes that want to be free of imperialism can join in the struggle to form a front of national liberation. Because of the feudal nature of these societies, the peasantry predominates over the industrial working class, so that the world strategy of having the countryside surround the cities is also the strategy for the liberation of a particular country.

These notions are plausible enough to gain wide acceptance. Compared to city people, peasants are poor. Imperialism is a historical fact, and industrial countries were imperialistic.

Even since the liquidation of colonies, the expansive tendencies of industrialism are almost irresistible. Governmental leaders of unmobilized countries seek resources from industrial nations and, to that extent, are dependent upon them. These ambiguous pieces of evidence are sufficient to persuade ambitious and ignorant people of the possibility of a great conspiracy of exploitation. This possibility often becomes a moral certainty because it gives both consolation and hope to the frustrated people of poor countries.

Communism in Thailand

In Thailand, Communist organizers have hoed an infertile row and harvested few beans. The first representatives of the Communist International seem to have arrived in Thailand in the late 1920's. They were refugees seeking sanctuary from the debacle of China. Among them was a major and ubiquitous figure in Asian Communist affairs, Ho Chi Minh. There is no evidence that this influx had much effect in the country. During the events of the constitutional revolution of 1932–35, some papers were circulated that suggested Communist influence but there was little more than that.

Communism became an issue in 1932, however, not because of the activities of any party but because Pridi Phanomyong (see page 81), the youthful intellectual leader of the People's Party, issued a utopian pamphlet entitled *National Economic Plan*. His plan was based on the idea of nationalizing all economic resources. It was promptly denounced by many people, including Pridi's military colleagues, as "bolshevism." This event had two important effects. One was that it set back Pridi's career and may have undermined, at a critical moment, the strength of the civilian faction. The second was that it led to an anti-Communist law that served as an effective instrument for the continuing suppression of Communists, as well as other dissidents. Whether Communism would have prospered without that law is very doubtful, but the existence of the law effectively foreclosed any such possibility in the prewar period.

There are four Communist Party organizations in Thailand. The most important is the Chinese Communist Party of Thailand (CCPT), which is a branch of the Party that rules the Chinese People's Republic. This Party branch operates in the Chinese community in Thailand. The second is the Communist Party of Thailand, which is thought to be an offspring of the CCPT and which was established to give a more national character to Communist Party activities in the country. The third organization is the Indochinese Communist Party (ICP), organized by Vietnamese in 1930 and formally dissolved in 1945. It seems to have reappeared, with national constituencies, in 1950. The ICP is reported, by some observers, to claim jurisdiction over not only Vietnam, Laos, and Cambodia but also over Thailand and Burma. The dissolution of 1945 is said to have been fraudulent and the aspiration for regional control, to be still active. In any case, this party, or its successors, has some position, at least among Vietnamese, in Thailand. The fourth is the Malaysian Communist Party, operating in southern Thailand.

The interrelations of these parties is, nevertheless, obscure. What is not obscure is that organized Communism in Thailand is feeble and dependent. All of the parties operating there are dependencies of other national parties and may be considered agencies of these other parties. This situation is a vicious circle, because the dependent parties find it impossible to develop political action designed for specific conditions in Thailand. Rather, their actions are derived from the foreign policies of Communist China or North Vietnam. For this reason, the influence of the parties does not expand in Thailand, they cannot develop a base of power there, and, thus, they remain dependent. It is only a matter of speculation, but it seems likely that, in this time of crumbling control systems within the Communist movement, the mother parties are as much concerned to maintain control of the local daughter parties as they are to see local influence expand.

The basic policy framework within which the Communist parties have worked is that of front politics, with the aim of reducing American influence. The Communists' political strategy, which derives from the assumption that they are always a minority, is a matter of two questions: (1) With what other groups can an alliance be formed; and (2) will such an alliance be through the leadership or with the rank and file of the other groups? In Thailand, the answer to these questions has varied, and the strategy has varied from time to time, depending, apparently, on how the Chinese viewed the world.

Since the early 1950's, there have been three main phases. The first was to seek alliances with anyone opposed to the government, such an alliance being based on the issue of peace. "Peace" meant support for the position of the Soviet Union, China, and the Vietminh against the United States and NATO in Europe, against the United States, Japan, and Nationalist China in Korea and Taiwan, and against the United States and France in Vietnam. The organization of a special committee for the peace effort, in 1952, precipitated the decision of the government of Thailand to suppress the Communists and to strengthen anti-Communist legislation.

The second phase, occurring in the period 1955–59, was based on the idea of "peaceful coexistence." Alliances were sought with all groups, through their leaders, who would support the termination of SEATO and neutralism for Thailand. Even government leaders were not excluded from the possibility of alliance, and the strategy was aimed mainly at government policy.

The election campaign of the period permitted the organization of political parties and, in the end, a Socialist Front based on these notions. But the *coup d'état* of 1958, led by Field Marshal Sarit Thanarat, ended this activity in Thailand, while various events, in the world and in China, terminated the policy from the Chinese side.

The present phase, begun in 1961, is that of an alliance of all Communist forces, which intends to organize a war of national liberation, based in the countryside, to overthrow the government and drive out American influence. In this period, there has been a slow development of organizations and pseudo organizations operating in China and Vietnam, as well as clandestinely within Thailand. The Thailand Patriotic Front appears to be the basic organization. It was founded in early 1965 and received publicity from various Chinese and Vietnamese radio and news services. The Front is ostensibly an alliance of various special groups, such as the Thailand Independence Movement, Thailand Federation of Patriotic Workers, Thailand Patriotic Young Organization, Thai Afro-Asian Solidarity Committee, Liberation Farmers Party, and others. Whatever existence these organizations may have in Thailand is secret, since the government has arrested such workers as they can find.* The personalities associated with these organizations abroad are men and women of minor political position, some of whom have been active in such work for many years. The most important figure is Pridi Phanomyong. Pridi has been a prominent figure in Thai politics since 1932. After a hectic career, he was forced into exile in 1947 and has been a resident of China since 1950. He is an old man and the last survivor of the "Promoters of the *Coup d'état*," a group vaguely equivalent in Thai history to the American Founding Fathers. He has not been officially associated with any of the above organizations, but his name and voice occasionally issue from a Chinese radio station. While his name is still well known in Thailand, it is not

---

* Three major arrests have been reported since 1961. One was the arrest of Krong Chandawong and a group operating in the far northeast region (see above). The second, in 1962, was the arrest of Ruam Wongphon and a group operating in the central region. The third, in 1967, was the arrest of a number of obscure people in Bangkok, said to be the Central Committee of the CPT.

likely that he has any organized following. In short, neither in terms of leadership nor organization does it seem that the liberation movement has a useful base within the country.

Vulnerabilities

In any description of power in Thailand, the weakness of the revolutionary organizations must be emphatically juxtaposed with the strength of the government. For revolutionary war to succeed, as it has in China, Vietnam, Cuba, or Algeria, the movement must penetrate, in an active, organized way, the pattern of existing authority. It must develop an organized authority that either replaces the previous authority or, by some novel organization, blocks the operation of the existing authority. In China and Vietnam, the revolutionary movement developed its organization when the Japanese occupation had swept authority away by massive force. It is probable that, in South Vietnam, the organization had been in operation since before 1954. In Algeria, the clear-cut issue of colonialism, the presence of a large, exploitative European population, and the failure of French will provided a combination of conditions that undermined French authority. The Cuban experience is the most suggestive for the situation in Thailand, although even here the analogies are ambiguous. The broad and enervating grip of the sugar interests had demoralized the population, while the brutal, repressive actions of Batista's regime undermined the weak foundations of his government's moral authority.

There is not sufficient space here to review the history of revolution in the world. Nevertheless, it is true that governments are overthrown when they cease to work effectively and with some modicum of justice. This breakdown can come about because of defeat in war, or occasionally because the government does not adjust to great social and economic changes in the country. Neither of these situations exists in Thailand and, with some attention, they will not.

We, of course, cannot assume that Thailand will not be defeated in an international war. It is not completely within the power of the Thai Government or the United States and other allies to prevent China or Vietnam from invading Thailand. Nevertheless, this contingency has been the basis of SEATO and other military planning. These efforts have reduced the possibility of invasion to a very low point and the possibility of defeat to approximately zero. Thus, we can rule out further consideration of defeat as a form of disruption. Moreover, if we look at the cohesion of the country's ruling class during the quasidefeat of 1945, we see a remarkable capacity for sticking together at such a time.

The social and economic tendencies that might disrupt authority are there. The thrust of economic development is bringing new social relations and new classes into existence. New roads and markets not only release productive activity but also political activity. People engaged in commerce and industry, even in foreign trade, are concerned about investment patterns, tax policies, sound money, honest weights, fair enforcement of contracts, certain land tenure, and genuine protection from fraud, crime, and violence. Educated people are concerned about schools and hospitals. It is the change in their way of life that leads them to expect and demand further and more elaborate change. Thus, the demands upon government and the definitions of effectiveness and justice are being modified. This modification may amount to a disruption of authority, if the government fails to respond to it.

Thailand's government is strong as it faces the challenge of revolutionary war. Its mere existence as a continuous, complex, manageable and, truly nation-wide organization is its most powerful asset. A second asset is mobility, the capacity for adaptation, as demonstrated not only over the past century but, more specifically, in the reorganizations and innovations of the last decade. Against this resource, the efforts of the Thailand Patriotic Front and the Communist Party of Thailand seem feeble, if not pitiable. The machine of government is not free of defects as we can see from our discussion in this and the two succeeding chapters. Authority overconcentrated in the cabinet and office of prime minister, bureaucratic conflict and immobility, the perils of using corrupting methods to get action and cohesion, bad police practices, and monopoly power in the economy all enervate the government. But we need not blink at the defects and blemishes of the Thai Government to conclude that, relative to the genuine alternatives, it is strong and active.

At the present, revolutionary war has two possible entering wedges, both of which the Thailand Patriotic Front is trying to use. The first is ethnicity. Those areas where some militant action has been staged—the far Northeast, the northern hills, the extreme South, and the western border—are all places where distinct differences of language, culture, and background are found among the people. These differences are a basis on which to construct both cohesion and antagonism. The Thai Government's insistence on uniformity throughout the nation—an approach growing out of a determination to build a nation of homogeneous Thai people—was justifiable and reasonable. It worked for the most part, but failed to penetrate to the outer limits of the state and was attenuated in the peasant groups by the equally reasonable intention to avoid disrupting their indifference to politics. Economy of effort was the principal virtue of this approach to nationalizing the country. The new economic and political influences, however, require a much greater investment in responsive apparatus to manage the remaining differences without permitting these differences to serve as a basis for revolution. Even revolution on the geographical or social fringes can be expensive and resonant.

This leads to the second danger. In responding to the challenges of revolutionary war and, particularly, ethnic differences the government could fall into the trap of indiscriminate repression and heavy reliance on American support. Feeble efforts by the Thailand Patriotic Front have importance merely because of their Chinese and Vietnamese impresarios. If the government should take unwarranted confidence from its American allies and embark on increasingly vigorous and violent means of repressing the dissension, it could conceivably validate the accusation that it is a puppet of American imperialism and find itself at war with its own people.* The nationalism of the Thai people, while undemonstrative, is genuine. The authority of the government emanates, in large part, from the belief that it is a government of the Thai and is responsive to their needs. It has strong associations, in history and at present, with the King, the religion, and the safety and welfare of the country. If these associations were to become less firm, then the government would find it difficult to sustain its authority. So far, there is very little basis for imagining that this will develop.

But the basic threat of insurrection—a Communist-organized war of national liberation—is its possible effect on the core of Thai politics. Effective public opinion is mainly that of the urban bureaucratic and business classes. Their fate and future depend upon the ability of the government to fulfill its obligation to defend the country not only from hostile foreign influence, but also from destructive war. Particularly within the bureaucratic group, there is a large segment that is probably indifferent to whether the present regime or another, possibly Communist, regime is in power.

The Thai people, even the educated classes, are not an ideological people. Rather they are a pragmatic, but also a moral, people. Their loyalty and support depend upon the effectiveness of their leadership. If the still minor insurrectionary activity were to appear to grow despite the government's efforts to suppress it, this bureaucratic group could be-

* A suggestive example of this possibility is the use of airpower in the suppression of the Meo.

come seriously demoralized. The cohesion of the government could dissolve, and the political stability of Thailand could disappear in a welter of factionalism and lethargy. In that way, Thailand's political stability is genuine but fragile.

Within the framework of ideas common to Thailand's educated people the concept of nationalism, that is, independence from foreign domination, runs like a scarlet thread. The charges of the Thailand Patriotic Front that the government is merely the puppet of America are addressed to this nationalism. The presence of American influence, particularly troops, lends a certain plausibility to these charges. While the influence of America is substantial in the country, the government is, in fact, quite resistant to it. The plausibility of a charge, however, need not be entirely related to its accuracy.

VI

Politics in Thailand

Traditional Attitudes

Although more than 33 million people live in Thailand, the number who are in politics is very small. Of Thai adults, an overwhelming majority is not involved in politics. Most of these persons have a "we and they" attitude toward political matters. For them, politics is the business of the politicians, or, more broadly, of the ruling class and is something of a show that, as they see it, has little tangible effect on their lives. Perhaps "show" is not quite the correct term, because this attitude, an ancient one, is connected with a characteristic Thai view of the way the world works. *160403*

According to this view, the world is a web of moral relationships. All elements—things, people, actions—of the world, indeed of the cosmos, are related to each other in terms of power. The power of each element is determined by its virtue and moral value. The moral value of things is their true and essential nature and determines their relative place in the universe. This value results from acts of will, according to a principle of moral cause and effect, so that the universe is understood to be governed by will or, really, by the wills of many.

One result of this view of the world, the importance of which is difficult to exaggerate in the Thai situation, is the idea that a person's social place, in the human universe, is a result of his own will and that, in some way, he is ultimately

responsible for his own position in society. In the most traditional conception, the human world is but one of the worlds
in the universe. There also are the world of the beasts and
things, as well as the higher worlds of celestial beings. These
worlds, or levels, are locked together in one systematic universe.

The position of a being, human or otherwise, in this universe may be measured by the degree to which he is subject
to the will of others or has power over others. This conception
is the one which must be kept in mind in any discussion of
Thai politics, that is, the necessary and just unity of virtue
and power. Those who have power are good and deserve
power. Those who gain power are good and deserve their
good fortune. Power justifies itself. Although there is the possibility of degeneration to a cynical view that might is right,
the Thai concept is properly a magico-religious idea that
right is might.

In short, the world, as the Thai see it, is a hierarchy of
statuses and powers, ranging from this life and world through
all lives and worlds. The continuum of the Thai cosmos is not
that of space and time but rather of virtue and power. Ideally,
this cosmos is a just one and is ruled by an unbreakable law
of cause and effect, that is, right behavior leads to advancement in the hierarchy. But the most important aspect of this
conception is that the world is organized according to a principle of hierarchy of statuses. To these statuses are attributed
duties and power, and each has its moral qualities. Such statuses tend to be responsible to themselves or those above for
the proper behavior. This notion of the world as a hierarchy
of self-justifying power is the basis of the "we and they" attitude toward politics.

Along with such ideological factors, there are and have
been, over the years, certain more concrete social and economic factors, which have prevented any serious violation or
questioning of this traditional view and the attitudes that rely

on it. It is reasonable to assume that a good deal of stimulation is required before the average man (in Thailand or elsewhere) inquires seriously into the ideas he received at his mother's knee. The social and economic changes in Thailand during the past century developed in an indigenous and organic fashion, which absorbed the potential shock to the traditional view of society. It is not to be inferred from the following points that Thailand has seen no change. But such changes have not collapsed a traditional set of attitudes toward authority.

The society of Thailand today is, as it was a century ago, dominantly preindustrial—almost precommercial—*economically,* more or less neolithic *technologically,* and residually feudal *socially.* I would like to quote here from Ingram's *Economic Change in Thailand:*

> The Thai population has largely remained in agriculture, and has neither improved techniques nor increased the proportion of capital to labor. Moreover, most changes in the economy as a whole have been in volume rather than kind. New methods have not been used, new products have not been developed. No product of any importance (besides rubber) is exported today which was not exported in 1850.*

This quotation illustrates the truly striking fact that, between 1850 and 1950, a century of revolutionary upheaval, Thailand, in very substantial ways, remained the same.

The Farmer

There have been changes in the public life of the farmers, who presently constitute about 75 per cent of the population. The most important of these changes may well be the great improvement of internal and external security. Invasion ceased with the coming of British and French imperialism,

* James C. Ingram, *Economic Change in Thailand* (Stanford, Calif.: Stanford University Press, 1955), p. 209.

and banditry has been substantially suppressed through the development of a more effective police and interior administration. Secondly, land tenure was made more secure by the introduction of a system of individual free title to replace the traditional feudal system of usufruct. Thirdly, the personal obligation to serve the king or other officials for several months each year, an obligation which persisted from ages eighteen to sixty, was changed into a system of free wage-labor and ostensibly universal military service for a two-year period. Finally, after the revolution of 1932, direct taxes on peasants, such as the head tax and the land tax, were negligible, and the state has since derived its revenue from what are, apparently, less burdensome indirect levies. But, for the most part, the undoubted changes in the way of life of the Thai farmer—changes in marketing and crops, for example—have been of such a nature that they have apparently not disturbed his traditional sense of social organization.

Such changes have not seriously interrupted the traditional social organization for the following reasons. First, they have been gradual. The period of change from a more or less purely traditional Thailand to the present state has covered four generations. Second, the changes have been marginal, rather than central. For example, the effect of new opportunities to sell rice or other crops has been that the former subsistence-level farmer began producing for the market over and above his family needs, without allowing himself to become totally dependent on the market. Thirdly, the changes have included a reduction of life's uncertainties, as the government's administration increased the security of persons and property. Fourthly, their cost has been obscured by the shift of the base of wealth to profits from the newly developing international trade, whereas the trade itself affected the farmer only indirectly. Finally, from the point of view of the farmer, relations with authority have continued, without interruption, in the person of government officials.

The great bulk of the population of Thailand lives a relatively secure, stable, and economically tenable life, in which the government directly plays only a small role. Because of this situation, the peasant is not stimulated to inquire much into the basis of his traditional view of politics as "their" affair. It should be noted here, parenthetically, that there are, of course, elements that have made the interconnection of the government and the masses much closer and more delicate. Internal security, education, mass communications, and the increase to their living standard have become a part of the peasants' lives and depend on management by the state. The fact that the state's management has been adequate up to now is an important factor in maintaining the peasants' indifference to politics.

Certain signs of social, economic, and political discontent among the peasants, however, indicate the disruptive force of development and, perhaps, a threat of insurrection. Such signs may be interpreted as symptoms of a latent political consciousness. The symbolism of the wrist watches owned by farmers who have no need to know the time of day, fountain pens in the pockets of the semi-literate, glistening leather shoes, freshly starched white, broadcloth shirts, and permanent waves all suggest questing for more on the part of the peasantry. At present, whatever malaise this questing represents is only a potential political force. In spite of various attempts, no one has yet found the touchstone to realize it.

The Political Class

The character, experiences, and inner relationship of Thailand's political class have undergone substantial political change. In some metaphoric sense, this group has been required to absorb the brunt of change in order to maintain the effectiveness of traditions which support its position. From its own point of view, this class has been successful in absorbing changes along many lines and has been able to retain its power. For present purposes, let us look at the political class, its character, and the problems imposed by change, particularly in the political and constitutional realm.

The model for the political class in Thailand is a three-tiered pyramid. The top level includes several dozen people, who do, or could, dominate the ruling class and the country as a whole, by manipulation of various political forces. This group involves senior military commanders, a few men of outstanding reputations gained in the bureaucracy or in the subsequent interplay of politics, and, perhaps, two or three men around the throne. At any given time, there have never been more than a dozen such men in power, although the increased requirements of managing complex government activities tends to enlarge the group. The second level of the pyramid consists of about 1,000 persons, including senior officials and military officers of colonel and general rank, some princes, and, perhaps, some particularly powerful businessmen. Whereas the top group dominates, it is only through their manipulation and control of the second group that they gain, hold, and use power. The base of this structure is what may be called the political public. It is made up of educated and articulate citizens in Bangkok, the provincial towns, and, to a small extent, in villages, who interest themselves in the details of political activity. It is made up of high school and university graduates, who are, largely, in the bureaucracy, professional people, journalists and other writers, and members of the commercial white-collar group. This political class constitutes between 1 per cent and 2 per cent of Thailand's total adult population.

The organizing institutions of this group have been predominantly bureaucratic, in the broadest sense of the word. They are the military, the throne, the civil service, the National Assembly, and the business community.

Political power is generated by persistent cooperation of people. In Thailand, political power comes, very largely, from government organization rather than from such private institutions as parties, corporations, or special interest groups, because, among the Thai people, such cooperation is confined, almost entirely, to the government. For this reason, the Kingdom has been accurately called a "bureaucratic polity."

The Army, and, to a lesser extent, the Air Force and Navy are the organizations that generate the most power. Certain civilian organizations that are large or that control necessary resources are also important. For example, the National Police Department, the Department of Local Administration, and the Ministry of National Development provide significant bases of power.

When considering the Government of Thailand, therefore, it is necessary to appreciate not only the organization charts of administrative responsibility but also an overlay of political power that is the pattern of policy-making and action.

There are a large number of departments, the basic organizational units of the Thai Government. Each is charged with an area of responsibility, which is more or less broad but well defined. These departments are grouped together in twelve ministries: the ministries of Defense and the Interior are the oldest, largest, and most important. The other ministries are Foreign Affairs, Agriculture, National Development, Education, Finance, Economic Affairs, Industry, Public Health, Justice, and Communications.

The *military establishment* has taken upon itself the role of political mentor to the nation. By means of successful *coups d'état,* it has staked a substantial claim to political dominance, which it has enhanced by maintaining its financial, educational, and administrative autonomy. In addition, the fact that a substantial portion of the armed forces is based in the capital is a matter of no small political importance.

The position of the *throne* and the use of its prestige are rather obscure. Although it is maintained as a symbol of national unity, the royal power sank to almost nothing with the abdication of the seventh King of the Bangkok Dynasty in 1935. Since the breakup of the revolutionary group during World War II, however, it is clear that the throne is gaining in power and prestige. King Bhumibol Adulyadej, on the throne since 1950, has been playing an active political role. Because of his long tenure as well as his majesty, the government has encouraged and supported his role as an active symbol of national unity. But, by such activities, he risks jeopardizing the political neutrality of the crown.

The *civil service* lacks the unity and hierarchy of the military services. Such characteristics would be necessary for it to take a dynamic part in politics as a single organization. Within the civil service sphere, however, it is possible for a man to rise to a position of prominence and power, from which he may be drawn into the top group. At the same time, the cooperation of the civil service is vital to the ruling clique, because the civil servants have a fairly homogeneous social and economic outlook and are dominant in the political public. Before the ruling group can press any novel course of action, it must first lay the groundwork in this group.

The *National Assembly* has constitutional powers of legislation and interpellation. It is the institutional base of elected provincial politicians.* Because of the shadow of a powerful executive, backed by the military and the civil service, the Assembly has been developing a certain *esprit* among those members who have attained their positions through election skills. They seek to further their common interest, even though they are divided into voting groups and political parties. In general, each member must be elected through his own efforts, in his own province. Party labels are, to a large extent, incidental. The National Assembly has tended to take on the character of a separate political force within political life, because the governing group must have parliamentary

* The election of the National Assembly was discontinued in 1958 and reestablished in 1969.

support to maintain itself legally, while, at the same time, members of the Assembly must compete with military officers and bureaucrats for position and influence.

The Bangkok and national *business community,* like business communities everywhere, deals in policies on the level of influence. Although various industries, such as the rice merchants, are organized and occasionally consulted or admonished by the government, business influence moves mainly through individual connections. Because of the general (but not completely accurate) conception of the businessman as an alien, that is, Chinese, American, European, or Japanese, the community enters politics at something of a psychological disadvantage, even though the ethnic distinction is becoming less and less valid. For the American, European, and Japanese, this problem is, to a large extent, offset by diplomatic support, but, for the overseas Chinese, it is necessary to work out an accommodation. For the Thai political leadership, the problem of business is one of regulation. Because a substantial part of the state revenues derives from commercial activity—customs taxes, premiums on exports, and business taxes—careful regulation of business is vital to the state's stability. At the same time, the need of the businessman, particularly the Chinese, for some protection against heavy regulation makes political influence a premium qualification for successful business management. The opportunities for political and personal enrichment have not been overlooked by Thai political leaders. As the prime source of ready cash, the business community is a significant political force, but, since it has neither guns nor votes, it is manageable, in most instances.

Forces for Change

What are the dynamic forces for political change in Thailand? The pattern of change is often described as "change from above" or "administered change." Such a description of the pattern is partially accurate, in that the responsible authorities have usually sought to cope with pressures external to Thai society by making adjustments in its internal organization. But the idea of "change from above" is misleading, insofar as it suggests a theory of self-conscious façade building.

The latter idea should be discussed first of all. As one commentator has written, the "institutions of pseudodemocratic complexion that have been established and re-established in Thailand since the revolution of 1932 have been virtually meaningless."* The full implication of such a statement is basically nonsensical and extravagant. It would seem necessary to assume that the establishment and re-establishment of institutions over a period of a generation, in a nation which has demonstrated political skill, must have some meaning. It is true that the Thai are an exotic people and, therefore, can be expected to behave oddly. Nevertheless, it seems doubtful to conclude either that so many of them are so dull-witted that they have been engaged, all these years, in a great deal of meaningless activity, or that they are so wily that they have been manipulating a vast, expensive puppet show in order to confuse the world.

The process of "change from the top" also suggests a capacity for full control. The most interesting part of political change in Thailand during the past century has been the pattern of unforeseen consequences resulting from deliberate changes. The events of history are, of course, an unbroken web, but, for the sake of illustration, we may distinguish two series of events in which introduced changes led to unforeseen results.

In the latter part of the nineteenth century, as Britain and France marched on Thai territories in the valleys of the Mekong and Chao Phraya rivers and elsewhere, it became clear to the royal government at Bangkok that something had to be

---

* Richard Butwell, *Southeast Asia Today—and Tomorrow* (New York: Praeger, 1961), p. 53.

done. The government decided to attempt to gain control of the territory, its people, and its resources in a manner much more direct than in any previous government effort. A major element in the accomplishment of this end was the reorganization of the traditional bureaucracy along the lines of those nations which were threatening the Kingdom. Therefore, new and functional ministries were established; a territorial administration, patterned after British India, was developed; new financial arrangements were made, and so on. In order to operate this new system, it was necessary to train people in the new ways, most usually by sending them to Europe. As had been planned, one result of this effort was the development of a rather effective administration. Another result was the creation of a new class of technically expert bureaucrats, whose relationship to authority, mainly the throne, was different from that of the old bureaucracy. These people were, on the one hand, more dependent, because they were hirelings—paid officials—and, on the other hand, less dependent, because they were experts. In a very real way, they were less responsible and more self-confident. The results of this situation were, first of all, a state of tension, secondly, an alienation from traditional ideas of authority, and, thirdly, an acceptance of European ideas of constitutionalism. This brief account attempts to summarize the process by which the throne initiated a series of changes which ultimately resulted in its removal from power.

Now, it is to be noticed that the bureaucratic group utilized constitutionalism to remove the throne from power and may, thereby, have initiated a series of changes that could result in the bureaucracy being removed from power. That result has not yet come about, however. The bureaucrats are still in power, but they have been struggling with the consequences of their actions for more than three decades. Their major problems are the legitimacy of leadership and the leaders' capacity for control. The usual tendency of large bureaucratic organizations to resist control from outside is particularly acute in Thailand, because political power emerges almost solely from the government departments and agencies. On the other hand, the bureaucratic power is not legitimate as such, so that symbols of legitimacy are required for both the government and its leaders.

Political leaders are not chosen by the public. They thrust themselves on the country. The organizers and leaders of the three great *coups d'état*, of 1932–33, 1947–48, and 1957–58, have served as national political and governmental leaders. Because these three critical events were promoted from within the government, all political leaders of note have had official careers. The military character of the coups has strengthened the dominance of military officers. The three big coups produced three organizations which acted to perpetuate the exclusiveness of the group involved, to maintain it in power, and to set policy. The three shadowy groups—The Peoples' Party of 1932, The Coup d'État Group of 1947, and the Revolutionary Group of 1957—have been informal, unpublicized, and cryptic in their operations. Their irregularly held meetings have been secret, and the internal power struggles have been known only by leaks or by inference. Both The People's Party and the Coup d'Etat Group eventually split into irreconcilable factions, while the Revolutionary Group's position dissolved under the autocratic leadership of the late Field Marshal Sarit Thanarat. In the end, the control of these groups collapsed.

Within the framework of the institutions of government and such semiformal organizations, the personal clique is the basic unit of influence. Cliques are not a uniform kind of institution but only a more or less stable system of loyalties. The clique takes a variety of forms and is built on a variety of direct, personal relationships, such as those among family members, teachers and students, and the like. Larger political organizations, such as the People's Party or the Revolutionary

Group, are pyramided from these cliques. Cliques may also be extended beyond the purely personal tie by means of ability to reward followers with power, privilege, and wealth.

But the continuation of this kind of organization depends on the persistence of a political class homogenous in terms of outlook and aspirations. While the homogeneity of the Thai political class is striking, there are, nevertheless, discernible differences that may intimate a more complex political life in the future. Six distinct groups are worth noting.

→ *Senior Military:* As a group, the senior military consists of officers in the various services of general officer rank. The political elite of this group are the members of the revolutionary group that supported the coups of 1957.* As insiders *par excellence* of the regime, it is they who reap the big rewards of office, prestige, and wealth, and it is unlikely that, among them, there was any antagonism to Sarit's regime as such or that they oppose the continuation of the present form of the regime. On the other hand, the rivalry among men of this group, particularly for control of military forces and means for affecting succession, is a source of tension. Having suppressed most of the outside opposition to itself, the senior military has not been forced to maintain internal unity and, as a result, its internal cohesion is weak. As time passes, the group may become weaker, if Prime Minister Field Marshal Thanom does not provide a focus for its loyalties. Should the Prime Minister lack sufficient charisma, his successor will very likely come from this group, as he himself did.

Junior Military: The relationship between senior military and the junior military is a critical one in present Thai politics. Most of the senior military were trained in the 1930's after the revolution of 1932 and moved into positions of high authority in the late 1940's and 1950's. Their outlook is

* The events that resulted in the regime completely dominated by Field Marshal Sarit Thanarat involved two coups. The first, in September, 1957, overthrew the leadership of the Prime Minister, Phibun Songkhram. The second, in October, 1968, abolished the constitution.

doubtless heavily affected by the nationalist phase of the late 1930's and the disappointment of World War II. The younger men are of the generation of the cold war and the emerging nations. Much of their training has been influenced by the U.S. military-aid program that has brought many rapid changes to the Thai forces.

One consequence of their training is a compounding of the tension that exists between generations in any occupation. The younger officers consider themselves to be more professionally qualified than their seniors to lead a modern combat force. Moreover, the juniors are embarrassed that, in many circles, there are doubts about whether the Thai forces will fight, if the necessity arises. They believe that the question exists as a result of the political preoccupations of their seniors. As professional soldiers, the younger officers assume that the army should fight, if need be; they accept the validity of the question, but they resent that it should be valid.

The reputation for corruption of the senior Thai military also distinguishes them from the juniors. The attitude of the junior officers toward corruption is, no doubt, ambiguous. They want either to be rewarded more adequately from the spoils or to have the corruption stopped. Regardless of the ambiguity, the persistence of corrupt practices among the senior military raises tensions in their relations with the juniors.

Finally, there is at least some sentiment in the Thai military, and particularly among junior officers, against the heavily political role of the military. This sentiment is ingenuous and rather a formality, but it does constitute a source of tension in the military forces. The significance of the sentiment lies in the tension it creates. Its existence also raises the question of the future relationship of civil and military elements in the Thai political system. The question is complex, because the present relationship is complex.

The position of the military rests largely upon the superior organizational strength of the military, relative to any comparable civil organization. Since military leaders have superior power, they are able to put themselves into office. With both power and the authority of office, they can organize a government which is constituted of *both* military and civil officials. So long as the military is the most organized force, there will be a certain inevitability to this structural relationship regardless of the sentiments of the officers.

Senior Civilians: The senior civilians are generally in a position of supporting the military power group by virtue of their technical skills and, to some extent, their reputations for integrity. For the most part, they hope to accomplish their objectives within the framework of military power. The most dynamic among them were made hopeful by Field Marshal Sarit's ability to get things done. At the moment, no doubt, a sort of suspension of judgment obtains among them, but, other than withdrawal from the regime, this group has no basis for independent action.

Bright Young Men: Within the civil service, there is a group of men up to the age of about forty, who are of considerable significance. These men form the postwar generation of officials, who have been relatively well trained (many of them in the United States and Europe) and are now entering important jobs in the universities and government organizations. This group is ambitious, energetic, and self-conscious. These young men, like the younger military officers, are antagonistic to the corruption and politicization of the senior military, but they supported the movement of Sarit's regime in the area of national development and will support his successor, if he demonstrates the necessary drive in that direction.

All of the foregoing groups are elements of the regime and constitute the central core of the political system. They, together with the great bulk of the bureaucracy, run the country. Insofar as they remain together, the regime of Field Marshal Thanom Kittikachorn, like Sarit's, can be accounted strong. As has been pointed out, however, there are tensions in this structure. The constellation of forces has the adhesive of power to hold it together. At the same time, the government is not free of opposition, which provides some centrifugal force.

The Royalists: One opposition group is that of the royalist conservatives. They hope that the influence of the monarchy can be enhanced sufficiently to eliminate corruption and get the military out of politics. This group adheres to a policy of constitutional monarchy and would like to see a parliamentary regime, dominated by a conservative upper house. The strength of this group lies in their prestigious social position, their supposed incorruptibilty, and their articulateness. Their leader is Seni Pramoj, a former Prime Minister.

The Socialists: The second major opposition group is the socialists. This is an amorphous collection of politicians, intellectuals, and students. Their principal claim to fame, at present, is that many of their more prominent spokesmen either have been in jail or are now in exile. Although the socialists are a politically marginal group, their appeal lies in an attractive, because purportedly progressive, alternative to the established regime.

It is difficult to assess the potency of the opposition. If we look at the make-up of the National Assembly's lower house, which has 219 seats, we see that, in the 1969 election, the Democrat Party of the royalist conservatives won 57 seats. (This party had captured the government of the City of Bangkok in a municipal election in 1968.) At the same time, 15 members of that same lower house are of left-tending parties. Electoral strength, however, is but one inconclusive measure of political significance in Thailand. Personal status and connections, rather than the size of a political party or its constituency, are the primary source of political and social influence for those outside the government.

In the past decade, within this political milieu, various methods of control—organizational, political, and constitutional—have been sought. Field Marshal Sarit, who became Prime Minister in 1958 and died in 1963, was the principal innovator in this search.

In terms of organization, he developed both the office of Prime Minister and the position of Supreme Commander. Since 1933, the Prime Minister has been, consistently, the most powerful position in Thailand. But, in the period of Field Marshal Sarit, changes, both legal and administrative, focused decisions on the Prime Minister, making the position uniquely potent and crucial. The Field Marshal was willing to take forthright action on a number of matters and both sought and had thrust on him organizational control over a wide variety of activities. During his tenure as Prime Minister he served as the center of administrative dynamism.

It was in Sarit's time that the concept of the Prime Minister as chief executive, rather than as first minister, developed. The analogy for this is the American Presidency rather than the British-Continental office of Premier. Along with the concept, a new organization somewhat like the Executive Office of the American President was developed within the office of the Prime Minister. In an attempt to gain control over the government, the agencies of control and information—the Budget Bureau, Audit Council, National Economic Development Board, and the agency for Central Intelligence—were created, if nonexistent, and gathered together, so that the burden on the Prime Minister increased steadily. Administrative congestion developed, because of a shortage of responsible people to keep the machinery working. Sarit, by virtue of his powerful personality, infused energy into the operation, and the few people close to him became overburdened, with positions on commissions, councils, and committees. After his death, much of the quality of focus was lost, as the agencies recaptured their autonomy.

Similarly, Sarit used his position as Supreme Commander of the Armed Forces to maintain some control over the military organization. The military services appear to be impervious to intervention, particularly in critical questions of command assignments and troop deployment. Although Field Marshal Sarit and, following him, Field Marshal Thanom, Supreme Commander and Prime Minister since 1963, have had influence on what happened in the services (particularly in the army since they both rose though army careers), the Supreme Command has been an ineffective organization.

To supplement such organizational devices, Field Marshal Sarit personally assumed a number of positions that he considered necessary to maintain some control over critical organization. The chart on page 117 shows the main jobs he held at the time of his death in 1963. By this means, he sought to substitute his own energy for the cohesion of a political group. This method, however, could not continue after his death, and these positions are now held by three military officers—Field Marshal Thanom Kittikachorn, General Praphat Charusathien, and General Prasert Rujirawong—and one civilian, Pote Sarasin, Minister of National Development. In short, changes of organizational charts have not been completely adequate in gaining control over the agencies of government. Although Field Marshal Sarit, because of personality characteristics, moved a distance along the road of infusing life into control organizations, his successors have reverted, at least part way, to a pattern of interorganizational negotiations.

The problem of control, however, is only in part a matter of power and organization. Legitimacy, the acceptance of authority as justified by law and right, is a fundamental aspect of control as well. In Thailand, the bulk of the population—mainly the farming population—accept the government as legitimate, because of the traditional conception of the world as a moral hierarchy of power. But within the political class, legitimacy of the leadership is at issue, because the constitutional question is unsettled. The Constitution of 1968 is one of many attempts to establish a fundamental law setting forth procedures and assigning power to elements of the government.

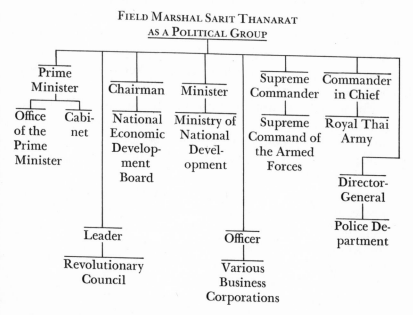

This constitution, while re-establishing elected representatives, is conservative in character. The main matter of contention in the constitutional order of Thailand has been the structure and role of the National Assembly.* In the Constitution of 1968, the National Assembly is bicameral. One house, the House of People's Representatives, is elected. Members are chosen by provincial constituencies (71 in all) on the basis of one member per 150,000 population. Each province has at least one member. The total of members in the first election, held in early 1969, was 219.

The second house, called the Senate and appointed by the King, with the approval of the government, is composed of

* See below, pp. 118–19.

"qualified persons eminent in science or other affairs" who are at least forty years old. The total membership of the Senate is three-quarters the size of the House. Members serve for six years with half of the Senate renewable every three years.

The National Assembly has legislative power and power to interpellate the government and to vote its confidence or nonconfidence in the government. Legislation normally passes both houses. The House of People's Representatives has superior power, because a bill can become law over the objection of the Senate if, after a waiting period, it is reaffirmed by the House. The power to vote confidence or nonconfidence resides in the National Assembly, as a whole, rather than in the two houses separately.

In sum, the power of the government over appointments to the Senate provides assurance of overwhelming influence in the process of legislation and in the relations between the cabinet and the Assembly. In this way, the constitution recognizes the fundamental source of political power in the Kingdom as separate and distinct from elections.

The constitution justifies the rule of bureaucrats and protects their position against a challenge from the throne. Nevertheless, the idea of egalitarian, representative government (whether it is genuinely or opportunistically adhered to is of no consequence here) is embedded in the constitution. The National Assembly, as the institutionalization of the egalitarian ideal, is, therefore, a base for challenging the bureaucratic leaders from the direction of popular representation. Because the primary allegiance of a national assembly is toward its electorate, it is resistant to less subtle forms of authority. The members rest on their own bases of power. As a result, they show a tendency toward insubordination that is sufficient to dishearten a bureaucrat and are a source of trouble. In previous parliaments, particularly in the 1950's, their stentorian demands have been calmed only at a high price in offices, privileges, or direct bribes. Moreover, the control of this undisciplined element was sufficiently difficult to warrant the closing of the Assembly.

Up to the present, however, the ruling bureaucrats have not dared—perhaps not even desired—to abolish the National Assembly. Their means to power, the *coup d'état*, is irregular, and their legitimacy is open to question. In order to gain legitimacy, the trappings of constitutional government must be maintained, and the National Assembly is one of these trappings.

Although the National Assembly has never been able to exercise fully its specific constitutional power to control the government, it has, nevertheless, become an important element of the political system. In the three decades since its establishment, its existence has been so fully institutionalized that it is difficult to see how it could be permanently abolished. If it is true that constitutional government legitimizes the present system, then the Assembly is indispensable. Moreover, it serves certain functions, beyond the mere symbolic, in the operations of the system. Although it has often been buffeted about in a most undignified fashion by irritable ruling groups, the Assembly's place has always been reaffirmed, and its ultimate legitimacy has not been questioned.

Nevertheless, the elected National Assembly symbolizes one major tension in the present state of affairs. When viable, it is the focus of the rulers' problem of creating new forms of political organization by which they seek to maintain their control.

Field Marshal Sarit was a confirmed anti-democrat. During his tenure as national leader, he argued publicly against democracy, on the grounds that it was inefficient and unsettling. Because of these characteristics, democracy, he believed, constituted a threat to development and security, goals of higher value than democracy. But Field Marshal Sarit never succeeded in persuading the political public, so that his attitude was effective, but temporary. Whether the new constitution will lead to another cycle of conflict between the elected and the bureaucratic groups remains to be seen. The government intends to continue its two-pronged policy of development and security. It also remains faced with the tensions of development, corruption, democracy, and repression.

VII

Corruption, Democracy, Repression, and Development

Corruption

It is striking that, as the unmobilized underdeveloped countries change to face the challenge of the contemporary world, governments often become corrupted.* There is nothing accidental about this phenomenon. As the society changes, the old ways are no longer sufficient for control of corruption, and new ways must be found. So it is, to a degree, in Thailand. The reasons for various sorts of widespread graft and corruption are to be found both in ways of thinking that remain from an earlier and different situation and in attempts to solve problems that result from the character of Thailand's political life. These two sources of corruption are related to each other, because existing methods are often used in seeking solutions to new problems.

In the days, more than a century ago, before Thailand began its internal adaptation to imperialism, the government consisted of the monarchy and its servants, organized in a sort of bureaucracy. The fundamental activities of the government, aside from important ceremonial and religious demonstrations, concerned defense, law and order, and revenue-raising. A host of high officials was responsible for these activities in certain regions, provinces, or cities. These officials

* Willem Frederik Wertheim, *East-West Parallels* (The Hague, Van Hoeve, 1964), pp. 101–31.

were granted rather wide discretion to do what was necessary for defense, civil peace, and taxation. In regard to revenues, officials received no salary and were expected to pay their own expenses, maintain their own establishments, and, also, send some income to the capital. In short, the traditional system recognized no distinction between public and private as far as officials were concerned, and, therefore, corruption—the use of public funds for private ends—was conceptually impossible. It was possible for an official to be just or unjust, liberal or oppressive, but he could not be corrupt.

In the past hundred years, the government has been completely reorganized, and financial methods have been changed. Officials are now civil servants and receive regular and established salaries for their work. Work is carried out within a framework of rules and regulations enforced by inspections and various disciplinary proceedings. Finances are regulated by a unified budget and audited by a central auditing council. Nevertheless, the traditional attitude that an official might expect to receive some remuneration from a citizen seeking a specific service persists. Moreover, the opportunities for graft are great in a state that provides a very broad variety of services and enforces a range of laws. Control machinery, if not supported by general social compliance, is always limited in its effect. Thus, petty bribes and extortions are not uncommon in Thailand.

Nevertheless, there are certain ethical standards which are maintained by informal as well as formal devices. The principal standards are that (1) services must be performed, and mere extortion is unacceptable and (2) misappropriating public money will be punished. The most common grounds for discipline against civil servants—discipline that can, and does, result in expulsion from the service—is financial delinquency. The existence of these standards indicates that such delinquency is a problem and that it is not complacently accepted.

A second source of corruption, or apparent corruption,

arises from efforts designed to overcome other obstacles to effective government. The Thai Government operates in a society that puts very little pressure on it. The National Assembly is very weak. There are no effective political parties, industrial, labor, or farmer pressure groups, potent local self-governments, or other organizations that generate power to move and influence government. Influence is exerted, but it is very specific and tends to go to the top, that is, to the cabinet or the Prime Minister. In this situation, the problem facing the leadership of the administration is how to maintain enough control both to prevent departments from doing the wrong thing and—what is as important and more difficult—to get them to do the right thing; in short, how to make the bureaucracy operate effectively.

Part of the solution lies in Thai civil servants' respect of and response to simple authority, and part to routine discipline. Thai people, in general, and civil servants, in particular, are very responsive to the authority of superiors, whether they be superior in social class or rank. Thus, orders and regulations from supervisors in the civil service—the Prime Minister, cabinet ministers, department heads—are very likely to be obeyed. At the same time, morale and *esprit de corps* in the civil service—or, at least, part of it—are sufficiently great to support a tendency to do the job.

Nevertheless, the bureaucracy—because of its isolation from external influence and because there are few organizations outside it in which a man can fulfill his ambition for power or for accomplishment—is the place where politics take place. Men strive to rise, make a reputation, implement a policy. But the organization of the bureaucracy is formally established. Ranks, promotions, and pay are set by law and practice, and there is very little flexibility within this framework. Therefore, something must be added to make politics —the organization of groups to support a man or a policy— possible.

What is added is favoritism, nepotism, bribery, and corruption. Men with political ambitions use these techniques to build cliques, factions, or parties that will respond to their will. The higher the man is, the larger his requirements. The more determined he is to implement a policy, the higher the cost.

What he does is supplement, with his own system of incentives, the flat and inflexible system of organization in the bureaucracy, which is characterized by low salaries, promotion by seniority, and established routines. He chooses the people most likely to assist him in his aims—whether they be clever, competent, or merely loyal—and favors them with special opportunities and gifts, in return for their help and support.

The evil of this sort of situation is that it operates, without any clear checks or controls, in secret and dark ways. Whatever controls there are lie in the mutual competition and watchfulness of the participants. So far, such controls have imposed and maintained limits within boundaries that can reluctantly be considered acceptable. Such a judgment is difficult to make, finally, because there are no clear standards. Nevertheless, certain plausible standards can be suggested, although, because of the secrecy inherent in the system, they are difficult to apply.

One such standard is an economic one: Does the transfer of money lead to the growth of the system as a whole, or is wealth being taken away from the whole community? This standard relates to the famous matter of numbered Swiss bank accounts. If the money that comes into the hands of officials and others by irregular means is sent out of the country rather than reinvested or redistributed within, the balance of judgment must be that the system is destructively corrupt.

A second standard is an ethical one: Does the transfer of money lead to some service being performed; is it really the price of something useful? This standard asks, is bribery a commission, or is it extortion?

A third standard is a political one: Does the transfer of money destroy or increase the government's cohesion and capacity to perform? When a department head develops, through favoritism, a clique of supporters, does he use this clique to further the accomplishment of the department's work or to pursue some private goal?

By all these standards, Thailand's government can be judged to be more on the constructive, rather than destructive, side. The effectiveness of the Thai Government, at least by comparison with its neighbors, is very great. When a job is established, it is generally completed. If money is appropriated for a building or a road, these things are built. If a new program—malaria control, rural development, cigarette manufacture, oil refinery, curriculum reorganization—is started, progress is made.

Nevertheless, the operation of a government or any organization by such a system of corruption, favoritism, and bribery is dangerous. It leads to a tolerant state of mind and is as perilous as drinking whiskey. Its balance of constructive, rather than destructive, effects is delicate and depends heavily on the morale of the users. Social drinkers, who normally drink only to relax after a hard day at the office, may, under stress, take to the bottle before lunch and end up as alcoholics. The outcome depends on the situation in which they operate, their view of the future and its possibilities, as well as the changes in the society. Such changes may, in the end, permit them to abandon the habit and drink milk.

Democracy Versus Repression

The persistence of corrupt practices is related to the weakness of democracy and the domination of leadership by the military. This latter situation has led some to call Thailand a "virulent, military dictatorship." From the point of view of Americans, democracy means constitutional representative government, more or less in the style of the United States. There are, of course, problems in judging the practice of one country by the ideal standards of another, particularly when their histories are very different. It is true that Thailand has no constitutional representative government in the American style, but democracy is a prized, if not universally held, aspiration of the Thai people, and much effort has been expended, over the years, in devising a workable representative government.

In 1932, a group of civil servants and military officers revolted successfully against the monarchy, which had, in the previous sixty years, built a centralized government by absolutist means. The revolt was aimed at the absolutism of the monarchy, rather than at the institution of a king or the centralized organization. A democratic, parliamentary monarchy was established by the constitution of 1932 and the first National Assembly was elected in 1933. While this revolutionary settlement succeeded in limiting the authority of the king by constitutional means, it failed to set up a permanent, workable representative government. In 1968, the fourth or fifth (depending on how you count) "permanent" constitution was promulgated. Election of another National Assembly, under another set of rules, followed in 1969. (See Chapter VI.) Until today, however, this effort has had defective results, and, for decades, the government has, indeed, been dominated by soldiers.

The reasons for this dominance are to be found in the character of political power. Power comes most frequently from the cooperation of groups of people seeking common ends. The more effectively the efforts of the group can be deployed to do what is necessary to reach the common end and, of greater importance, the more persistent the cooperation in seeking a variety of ultimate and intermediate goals, the more power is generated. Many social and cultural practices affect the capacity to cooperate, and such practices are different in different communities. It seems to be true that people in a particular society recognize only some forms of cooperation as feasible and legitimate. The cause for this may be found in the persistence of certain notions, often learned in childhood, of the "proper" principles of obligation and responsibility.

In Thailand, the dominant principle for generating cooperation is that of the authority of "superiors" over "inferiors." The Thai ideas of social relations force recognition of social rank, most clearly defined by the governmental system of ranks. For the most part, the Thai believe that persons of lower rank are obliged to follow the will of persons of higher rank; at the same time, people of higher rank are responsible for the protection and welfare of their followers.

One could say, with equal inaccuracy, that Thai believe all men are unequal, whereas Americans believe all men are equal. Neither proposition about equality is true in all circumstances; and neither do the Thai nor Americans believe their propositions to be completely true, nor do they act on the belief in all situations. Some such belief is useful for defining relationships between people in a society, but tensions necessarily develop, because, often, what people actually do conflicts with what they believe. I leave the reader to find examples of such conflicts in American life.

One such conflict in Thailand has taken place in the attempt to organize a representative National Assembly to control the administrative bureaucracy. Representative government is, at least in the twentieth century, based on the idea of equality—one man, one vote—as well as on the notion of accountability. Electors are equal, representatives are equal, and the representative is accountable to those who elected him. But, in Thailand, equals have difficulty cooperating, and superiors are thought to be responsible for, not accountable to, their followers. Thus, neither in the Assembly nor among the electors, has cooperation generated power. Members of parliament have behaved as more or less self-responsible figures, accomplishing what they can by wit, bargains, and temporary alliances. At the same time, electors have found no effective means, such as political parties, to call them to account.

In contrast, organizations of the government—ministries, departments, and, particularly, the military services—have been able, using rank and authority, to generate great power. In the United States, such things have happened, and departments of the government have been able to resist the control and scrutiny of either the Congress or the President, but rarely both. But, in Thailand, the power of the goverment departments, in relation to the National Assembly—a power based on tradition, hierarchy, and law—is overwhelming. Members of parliament, out of necessity, have had to join in the play of politics and power within the structure of the bureaucracy by becoming members of personal cliques and party-like groups, which when combined, approximate the strength of the government organization in question.

Another characteristic of Thai society that contributes to the difficulties of representative government is the weakness of constituent communities. The old Kingdom of Thailand, before the modernizing transformations of the past century, was made up of many city communities, that is, cities or towns, which were the focus of both secular and sacred life and which had a population of dependent peasant farmers. These communities might have served as effective constituencies in a system of representative government somewhat similar to boroughs, in early British parliamentary history, or states and towns, in American history.

However, the centralization and uniformity imposed by the reforms of recent Thai history weakened, where it did not destroy, much of the basis of these communities. Local princes and notables were suppressed and replaced by salaried servants of the King—all in the name and interest of security and progress. By the time of constitutionalism, the strength of the

communities was dissipated or captured by the central administration. Such communities have not, therefore, provided a
source of power for guiding the selection of representatives,
nor for calling them to account.

By contrast, the departments of the central government
have retained or even enhanced their power. It is from these
organizations that leadership, both of men and of policy, have
come. Among these many government organizations, the military and, particularly, the army have been the best organized,
the easiest to deploy, the most powerful. It is perhaps not a
surprise that the politics of the country have been dominated
by soldiers for most of the past thirty-eight years.

But is Thailand a "virulent military dictatorship?" This
question raises a specious problem but, nevertheless, represents a quest for some means of judging the value of a system
of government. Presumably, a virulent military dictatorship
is a government characterized by indifference to the will or
wish of the population, a government that, rather arbitrarily,
dictates to the people what they will do. Such a government
enforces its dictates by using violence (and not just enforcement) against its own population and guides its policy by the
aim of enhancing the power and wealth of the soldier through
military adventures. Finally, such a government presumably
poisons the community by its actions, ultimately bringing
about its decline and extinction. Perhaps the most plausible
examples in recent times are Germany and Japan in the
1930's and 1940's. Thailand, under its soldier-leaders, even
when they modeled themselves on foreign dictators, never
quite reached the evil of Nazi Germany or imperialist Japan.
Given its limits of resources and ability, however, the government of Thailand, between 1938 and 1944, extended itself
well into the realms of military adventure and internal repression. Its model, its course, and its fate bore some resemblance
to the Italy of Mussolini.

It is, perhaps, rather quaint to allude to such an old-fashioned figure as Mussolini. Yet it may not be without contemporary relevance. The use of historical parallels is risky when analyzing politics, but certain kinds of social problems recur in different places and times, and ways of responding to them may have similarities. Unmobilized societies in the process of change tend to produce political conflict, which is uncompromising and even extremist. This happens because of the weak links of obligation and responsibility between national politicians and the public. Politicians are often led to adhere to simple and dramatic positions of an ideological kind. Such a practice serves to amplify political utterances by rhetoric and to attract an indiscriminate, hopeful following. Both the weakness of internal political links and the tendency to ideology—often borrowed from world literature (for example, Jefferson, Mill, Marx, Hitler, or Mao)—invite influence from external power, which threatens, or is thought to threaten, national integrity. This situation, while enlarging political freedom, tends to inhibit the resolution of often pressing problems specific to the place. A countertendency, aimed at limiting political freedom for the sake of orderly resolution of problems, frequently develops. The fundamental tension of political life, the tension between freedom and order, becomes very stark. No simple manner of resolving this tension has ever been found, although philosophers and politicians have wrestled with it from Plato to Mao Tse-tung.

In Thailand, fear of disorder is never very far below the surface of political life. Thai people, at least among the educated political group, seem to feel that the world is a dangerous place, in which, if caution is not duly maintained, other people may quickly get the better of one. In the subbasement of Thai feeling about the world is the idea that everything is held together by the capacity of powerful figures. Among the less sophisticated, such figures may be magical or supernatural, but even the more educated believe that power orders the life of society and holds back an ocean of chaos beating at the shores of settled prosperity. Consequently, Thai political life is intolerant of the turbulence of political contests and has shown a preference for the order of administrative government, where conflict is resolved in the quiet of a committee room. This attitude, which is widespread but, of course, not universal, has lent support to the administrative approach to politics demonstrated by the military leaders of the past decades.

The governments led by field marshals have not been military governments in which the armed forces have displaced civilians in the operation of the government. On the contrary, these governments have been bureaucratic in the highest degree. If anything, the effect has been to make civilians of soldiers.

In the years of the constitutional period, there has been a persistent contest between the administrator and the parliamentary politician to set the style of political life. It has been an unequal contest, in which the parliamentarian has always been required to give way to the desire for order and the power of the bureaucrats. Moreover, many professed adherents to the style of parliamentary governments are administrators looking for a base of operations from which to improve their chances in the politics of the bureaucracy. The parliamentary tendency has, in this way, often harbored those who are weakly devoted to the development of parliamentary power. Members of parliament have also, not infrequently, succumbed to temptations of bribery, coming from within the government as well as from outside. Because parliament has never developed safeguards, either formal or informal, to limit the extent or effect of such temptations, the institution has been corrupted, even if many individual members are as honest as Caesar's wife. All of these tendencies have combined to undermine the morale of parliament, weaken its claim to power and respect, and give representative institutions a reputation for contributing to disorder.

Still, for some, a parliament remains as an object of ambition. This persistence has several contributing causes. One is political ambition. Although the bureaucracy provides an effective path for the ambitious, opportunities are limited to officials, either civil or military. Yet many ambitious and educated people are not in the bureaucracy. Intellectuals, provincial notables, schoolteachers, and lawyers have views and ambitions, but no opportunity for putting them forward. Such people uphold the virtue of parliamentary institutions.

Secondly, constitutionalists, who are concerned to preserve the termination of absolutism and limit the arbitrary character of bureaucratic government, forward the proposition that constitutionalism implies representative government. Such people may well not be democrats or liberals. Rather, they represent a quest for greater order, perhaps, but, in their case, greater order through law.

Finally, the idea of parliamentary government is closely associated with ideas of progress and civilization, which all people in Thailand value. In the eyes of the rest of the world —which the Thai, like so many people, feel to be attending closely to their behavior—and in their own eyes, no society is worthy of the name "modern" if it is undemocratic. Democracy, for the Thai, means freedom, substantial justice, and the end of privilege. As an abstract ideal, democracy is highly valued and often praised. For a truly democratic Thailand, an effective parliamentary government is necessary. At issue is the timetable for realizing this ideal.

Economic Development

In recent years, particularly during the regime of Field Marshals Sarit Thanarat and Thanom Kittikachorn, another modern value has come to the forefront—economic development. This regime has been a despotism of development, based on the fundamentally correct notion that economic growth requires social order. Democracy, with its tendencies toward disorder, is seen as threatening, if not inimical, to the process of development. Field Marshal Sarit spoke often of the need to lay the foundations of the economy and the society *before* democratic institutions could be established. With Sarit's death in 1963, his successor, Field Marshal Thanom, modified the stringency of this view, although it was not until 1968 that a new democratic constitution was promulgated.

The draftsmen of the new constitution have worked with the desire to provide representation, while checking the powers of the parliament over the government, thus limiting opportunities for disorder and the play of personal ambition. In the American style, for example, they have prohibited members of the legislative body from holding political office in the executive. They have restricted the power of parliament to overthrow the government. By legislation, an attempt is being made to reduce the number of so-called political parties to those groups which can demonstrate a capacity for competing in elections. Whether such a representative legislative body can find a firmer, although more restricted, position in the government remains to be seen. At the same time, development remains a central policy of the government of Thailand. The accomplishments of the recent past are too impressive to abandon. Moreover, the abstract objective of development is almost as attractive as democracy.

Economic development is, in fact, an array of problems. In Thailand, an examination of the economy can detect signs both to encourage and worry those who view development as desirable. A number of indicators of economic growth may be used, in any economy, as a basis for judgment and prediction. In Thailand, for example, increases in total production look very good as a rate of economic growth, less impressive in terms of quantities of dollars, not so good in terms of growth per person, and rather alarming if studied by section of the economy or region of the country.

Not many years ago, Thailand was an agricultural country *par excellence,* and its economy still relies principally on agriculture. More than 75 per cent of the working people are in farming, and many of the others are engaged in the transportation or processing of farm produce. The largest single item in the Kingdom's export trade is rice. Other exported farm commodities—rubber, maize, jute, and tapioca—if lumped together with rice, overwhelm exported products of mines and factories. Most of the commodities are produced by smallhold farmers producing substantially for their families and marginally for the commercial market. In short, Thailand is a country of peasant farmers—a classic underdeveloped, poorly mobilized country. The value of the per capita product of the Thai in 1966 was about $140. Nevertheless, Thailand's agriculture increased enormously in the past century, and, in the past decade, the rate of growth accelerated until 1967–69 when, for various reasons, it declined.

The growth of the agricultural sector has resulted primarily from three factors: (1) the availability of more capital for the sector, (2) improvements in agricultural technology, and (3) the development of a more efficient marketing system, which enabled previously subsistence farmers to raise cash crops. These three factors are obviously interrelated, and the importance of each varies in different locales and with different types of farming.

Although the agricultural sector has grown rapidly in the past century and, particularly, the past decade, its growth has been outpaced by other sectors and the economy as a whole. Not only is the agricultural portion of the gross national product declining, but the percentage of the population earning its livelihood from agriculture is also slowly declining. While agriculture is declining in relation to the rest of the economy, considerable diversification has occurred in this sector, specifically away from reliance on rice.

In absolute terms, the Thai economy is still backward, as

characterized by its over-all low productivity. But its perform-ance in this century, and particularly in the past decade, indi-cates that the economy is anything but stagnant. Even agricul-ture, the most backward sector, has demonstrated remarkable capacity for growth and change.

A brief look at the social side of economic activity will illuminate the character and problems of Thai economic life. Most of the Thai people, between 75 and 80 per cent, live on their own small farms, which are crowded densely in river valleys and flood plains. On those fields that flood every year, they grow rice, which is the only important crop that will grow in water. The farming villages support such institutions as schools and Buddhist temples. (The Thai are overwhelm-ingly Buddhist although some profess Islam or Christianity. These will, of course, support a mosque or church.) The household is the basic economic and social unit. The typical household is organized around an active couple, with their young children and, possibly, their semiretired parents.

The rice produced by the household will be used by the members, with the surplus going into the commercial market through a local rice mill. Other vegetable foods, as well as some poultry and livestock, may also be produced, and the use of these will follow the same pattern as rice. The Thai technique of rice production requires little capital, a few tools, and draft animals. In short, the Thai farmer is mainly concerned to produce food for his household, but, generally, he has spare time. Given a genuine opportunity for profitable production, the Thai farmer has demonstrated the will and ability to shift from subsistence rice-farming toward diversi-fied cash crops.

The character of this opportunity depends on several things. First of all, suitable land and water must be available. Generally, farmers are not willing to abandon growing their rice and turn to a completely commercial household economy. For the most part, cash crops are grown either on higher land that does not flood or, in the dry season, on rice land. Controlled water is often required. Secondly, because farmers are unorganized small holders, they do not have the capacity to develop markets for their commodities. Consequently, they will produce cash crops in response to a market organized by other people, either traders or processors of the crop. Finally, in case capital is required for machines, fertilizer, insecticides, or seeds, farmers usually require assistance, usually in the form of credit and technical advice.

Production of many such cash crops has been developed—in some cases, on a spectacular scale. Feed corn, cassava (tapioca), kenaf (jute), sugar cane, peanuts, beans, garlic, chili peppers, and tobacco contribute substantially to national production as well as to the farmers' income. Tree crops—for example, rubber, coconuts, and fruit—also are important.

This element of commercial agriculture involves a complicated system of collection, transportation, processing, and marketing. These activities are all based in the many market centers, towns, and small cities of the countryside. If it is true, as it appears to be, that a substantial part of the increases in agricultural production results from dormant capability awakened by new market opportunities—rather than from changes in investment or technology—then the development of this system of realizing the opportunities through market organization is a critical element in agricultural growth. It will remain so until the production that is latent in surplus labor and land has been mobilized. The key to this effort, as well as to the working of the entire national economy and growth, lies in Bangkok.

This city of about 2 million people lies on the banks of the Chao Phraya River about 10 miles from its mouth at the Gulf of Siam. It is the ultimate switchboard of national life—economic, social, and political. Bangkok is the site of the government, the major universities, the principal religious institutions, the headquarters of finance, the corporations of the import and export trade, the terminals of transportation, and most manufacturing industries. For Thailand, it is rather like a fusion of Washington, New York, and Chicago. The planners, the plans, and the effective instruments of the economy are all to be found in Bangkok.

It was not until 1960 that a strategy for economic development was formulated—as the first six-year plan—although elements of it were in use before then. According to the plan, economic growth depends on private mobilization of effort and resources supported by public investment in what is portentously called infrastructure (mainly transportation, communication, power, and control of water). It must be protected by the government's fiscal and financial policies, which are designed to stabilize the value of money and encourage certain kinds of investment and which are guided by notions of national priorities.

Much has been spoken and printed on the subject of economic growth and how to bring it about. Opinions on proper strategies include the Stalinist type of forced, total, central-planning, aimed at revolutionizing the character of the economy, and overcoming obstacles by force; Nehru-style central planning with large public investment in the so-called key industrial capacity; the Burmese type of nationalization of all nonagricultural production and trade; and Thailand's use of public policy and resources to support private enterprise. The appropriateness of various strategies depends clearly on the objective that is sought and the assessment of opportunities and limitations in the situation at hand.

In Thailand's case, the objective is to achieve a rising standard of living without undermining political stability. The Thai Government's assessment of opportunities and limitations within their situation centers on the themes that export markets and foreign capital are highly accessible, that much productive capacity, particularly in agriculture, is latent and can be realized by investment in facilities, and that the enormous and intricate process of mobilizing and organizing this latent capacity is beyond the ability of the central planner or government and ought to be left to private enterprise.

So far this strategy of growth has yielded good returns. In the six years of the first plan (1960–66), over-all production (GNP) rose from $2.7 billion to $4.2 billion. The growth rate of domestic production was about 7 per cent per year. The growth of agriculture went ahead at an annual rate of about 5 per cent, while nonagricultural production increased at a rate of about 10 per cent per year. Perhaps most remarkably, prices, during the plan period, remained almost constant.

With an open economy, Thailand's foreign trade is fundamental to economic activity. During the plan period, trade grew from about $900 million to about $1.4 billion. An unfavorable balance of trade has been made up, principally, by inflow of public and private investment, including U.S. foreign aid and military spending. The increasing proportion of capital imports and the diversification of agricultural exports are both indicators of the dynamic character of the Thai economy.

These rates are all very high for an underdeveloped economy, but, in order to get a better—or less exciting—conception of their meaning, we must realize that these rates are applied to small quantities. If we look at the figures on a per person basis, we can see that production per person increased at about 5 per cent a year between 1961 and 1966. This rate of increase meant production per person rose from about $107 a year to about $140, that is, less than $6 per year. The situation might be compared with money in a Savings and Loan Association. An interest rate of 5 per cent is rather good, and a man with a million dollars can live on the income of $50,000 per year. But a man with a hundred dollars will find it difficult to depend on an annual income of $5.00. Nevertheless, the analogy is of limited meaning. A national economy has no alternative but to increase itself and a rate of increase above 5 per cent, if sustained, is considered very good.

Two other aspects of Thailand's situation dull the luster of its otherwise satisfactory economic growth. These are the population increase and the inequities among different parts of the Kingdom. Thailand's population is increasing at a rate of more than 3 per cent, that is, almost a million people per year. This increase means that the national product must be distributed among more people all the time so that the impact of growth is diminished to that degree. In fact, the production of rice, the basic food, is increasing at just about the same rate as population, although over-all economic growth, as has been discussed, is greater than population growth.

Whether or not the government should adopt a program to slow the growth of population has been an issue in Thailand for several years. The Deputy Prime Minister, General Praphat Charusathien, has said that he is generally opposed to such a program, while a number of articulate, if not so powerful, people have supported it. It is not a simple thing to predict either the future rate of population growth or the effect of a program of contral. Nevertheless, it is not difficult to see that, if the population continues to increase at a rapid rate, the Thai people will remain very poor for a very long time, even if the economy continues to expand. Religiously, socially, and psychologically, the Thai people appear to be very receptive to birth control practices, which are already widely used. Consequently, a program of public support would, very probably, be successful in reducing the birth rate and limiting population growth. If such were to be the case, the growth of per capita income would be, thereby, increased.

Regional Variations

The problem of unequal economic growth among the various parts of Thailand has important political significance. For several reasons, the Thai Government recognizes four regions in the country—North, Northeast, Central, and South. In 1966, actual per capita production and the average yearly growth rate of per capita production in the period 1960–66 were as follows: *

	North	Northeast	Central	South
1966 per capita production (*approx.*)	$100	$70	$230	$155
1961-66, Average annual growth rate of per capita production (*per cent*)	5.3	2.3	6.6	3.2

The differences among the regions are considerable. The especially large figures for central Thailand can be accounted for by the greater productivity of the nonagricultural parts of the economy and by the fact that that region includes Bangkok. The south, because of the large part played by rubber growing and tin mining and because of its special relationship to Malaysia and Singapore, has always had a higher level of economic production in terms of money. But the differences, shown below, in the importance of a region's agricultural production and its rate of agricultural growth reveal substantial economic inequalities, particularly in northeast Thailand.†

	North	Northeast	Central	GNP
Agriculture as a per cent of regional and national productions, 1966	48.2	48.9	22.6	33.4
Annual rate of growth (*agriculture*), *1961–66* (*per cent*)	8.7	3.8	6.3	5.0

We do not have statistical material that distinguishes the metropolitan area of Bangkok from the rest of the country, but the fact that more than 60 per cent of all nonagricultural and nonmining production originates in the central region gives us some notion of the economic concentration around

* Thailand, National Economic Development Board, *Regional Gross Domestic Product 1961–66,* January 11, 1968, mimeo., Part II, Table I.

† Ibid., Table II; *The Second National Economic and Development Plan* (1967–71), (1968) p. 14.

and in Bangkok. Actually the disparity between the metropolitan area and the rural areas is sharp and conspicuous.

These various inequalities demonstrate the discontinuities in national integration that affect the different regions. To a diminishing degree, Thailand is several economies linked loosely to each other. As different regions of the country become integrated, people and goods will move more freely. Such a free flow should tend to equalize the rates of growth and amalgamate these economies. One of the principal problems facing the government, along with raising national production, is to bring these economies together.

Conclusion

Economic change is a potent stimulant to general social change. The resulting modifications, affecting the relations among classes, regions, and groups, are certain to strain the ability of government.

The apparent conflict between development and democracy, which was perceived and proclaimed by Field Marshal Sarit, is made of both truth and falsehood, as is often the case with political ideas. Development requires considerable planning and rational division of resources among programs. At the same time, its success generates conflicts and resistance, which must be overcome. Representative government amplifies these conflicts and strengthens the potential of resistance. Because of the susceptibility of a weak parliament to external influences, not only from within society but also from abroad, such conflicts may develop into arbitrary and irrelevant obstacles, which would disappear only if parliament itself disappeared.

On the other hand, conflicts and resistance may reflect authentic disturbances in social relations, which require some attempt at resolution. Representation and representative bodies are ways to inform the society, the government, and the

politicians of the character and importance of such disturbances. Insofar as a parliament works well, it may be the
means to resolve conflicts peacefully. The Thai Government
relies heavily on administrative organizations to collect information, which are often ineffective in interpreting their information and delivering it. For this reason, a parliament may
well serve to further development by easing conflicts. For such
conflicts between new and old classes may change from verbal
exchanges into insurrection.

VIII

Foreign Aid and Political Development

Assistance from one country to another is as old as nation-states. In the period since the beginning of World War II, assistance by the United States has developed a variety of techniques. It has, of course, been one of the principal means by which the United States has sought direct influence in friendly countries.

The United States has been assisting Thailand since 1951. The assistance has come through two distinct channels: the Military Assistance Program (MAP), administered by the Department of Defense and implemented in Thailand through the Joint United States Military Assistance Group (JUS-MAG), and economic aid administered by the Agency for International Development (AID) and its predecessors and implemented by the United States Operations Mission (see Table II).

United States foreign assistance to Thailand has included a variety of efforts and forms. Military assistance includes technical assistance and training of Thai military forces, equipment and supplies, and construction of facilities. Economic aid has included technical assistance in a variety of areas: grants and loans for resources needed in jointly agreed projects, and loans of commodities to husband Thailand's foreign exchange. American economic aid from 1951 through 1967 totaled more than $500 million. The amount of military assistance in the same period exceeded $600 million (see Table II). To give an idea of the economic significance, we

TABLE II

U.S. Economic and Military Assistance to Thailand
(U.S. fiscal years—millions of dollars)

Program	1951-57	1958	1959	1960	1961	1962	1963	1964	1965	1966	1967	Total 1951-67	Total Less Repayments and Interest
I. Total Economic	149.2	25.9	58.9	25.9	24.3	47.6	21.9	15.1	41.4	60.4	37.0	507.6	461.5
AID and predecessors	145.2	25.8	44.9	23.8	24.2	35.8	15.5	11.7	38.9	42.1	31.0	438.9	423.9
Other†	4.0	.1	14.0	2.1	.1	11.8	6.4	3.4	2.5	18.3	6.0	68.7	37.8
Loans	23.9	1.8	34.7	2.0	–	22.0	4.9	2.1	20.6	14.9	-13.5	118.5	67.6
Grants	125.3	24.1	24.2	23.9	24.3	25.6	17.0	13.0	20.8	45.5	50.5	394.2	394.2
II. Military	221.6	19.7	18.0	24.7	23.9	39.1	68.5	52.7	36.4	40.7	46.9	592.2	592.2
Total Economic and Military	370.8	45.6	76.9	50.6	48.2	86.7	90.4	67.8	77.8	101.1	83.9	1,099.8	1,053.8

* U.S. Overseas Loans and Grants—Net Obligations and Loan Authorizations.

† Includes Export-Import Bank Loans, Food for Peace, and the Peace Corps.

Source: Statistics and Reports Division, Office of Program and Policy Co-ordination, Agency for International Development, *U.S. Overseas Loans and Grants and Assistance from International Organizations, Obligations and Loan Authorization, July 1, 1945-June 30, 1967* (March 29, 1968), p. 73.

might say that U.S. assistance during that period had a value of about two average years' exports. If military construction and operating expenditures connected with the Vietnam war are included, the total would be considerably higher.

The United States is not Thailand's only source of assistance. Other countries—Britain, Germany, Australia, Japan, for example—and international organizations, such as the International Bank for Reconstruction and Development, the U.N. Special Fund, and the Asian Development Bank, have all provided grants, loans, or technical assistance to Thailand.* In longevity and total terms, the U.S. effort has been outstanding.

But the issues associated with foreign assistance are not so much a matter of size as of the effect and effectiveness of the programs. Foreign assistance is not a matter of philanthropy in any simple sense of the term. The programs that constitute foreign assistance—military or economic, technical or capital—have objectives that directly or indirectly are deemed beneficial to or in the interest of the United States. But the appropriateness of these objectives to American interests may be, and often is, in dispute. At the same time, the effectiveness of programs in attaining such objectives may be high, or, on the other hand, may fall very far short of perfection. It is, after all, a world of imperfection, and American aid programs share in this quality.

In the United States, foreign assistance has gone through an evolution of understanding. Ideas about both objectives and

* Assistance from international organizations (principally the United Nations and the International Bank for Reconstruction and Development) since World War II had a cumulative total of $269 million through 1967. Assistance to Thailand from other countries had reached a total of about $10 million in 1964. Sources: Thailand, Ministry of National Development, Department of Technical and Economic Cooperation, *Thailand Facts and Figures*, 1965 and U.S., Agency for International Development, Statistics and Reports Division, Office of Program and Policy Co-ordination, *U.S. Overseas Loans and Grants and Assistance from International Organizations, Obligations and Loan Authorizations*, July 1, 1945—June 30, 1967; March 29, 1968.

the appropriate means to attain them have changed over the years. These changes have resulted from changes in the world, changes in the understanding of the world, and changes in appreciation of the possibilities of foreign assistance as a means of influence. This evolution has affected the character of foreign assistance in Thailand.

For many years, it was thought, in the United States Government, that foreign assistance should seek to enlarge the area of security by contributing to military strength and economic growth. The programs, whether military or economic, were based on the idea that what the underdeveloped nations lacked was resources—arms and capital. If these resources could be provided, then greater stability would come about, and the United States would be more secure from the threat of Communist power abroad.

It was recognized that the use of arms and capital required some techniques that would be novel in underdeveloped countries. Thus, both the military and economic programs acquired a technical assistance component developed from the Point Four Program, initiated in the administration of President Harry Truman.

In the thinking about all these elements, relatively little attention was paid to internal politics. Foreign assistance was first viewed as a kind of political eunuch within the recipient country. This point of view turned out to be inadequate, if not incorrect. It came to be recognized that the configuration of political power within a recipient country influenced the ability to use assistance to good effect. In response to this realization, an effort was made to develop an aid doctrine for distinguishing recipient countries in terms of their capacity for self-help, that is, their ability to make internal changes and to mobilize their own resources to enhance the effectiveness of assistance in the form of capital and arms.

But this concern with self-help and the capacity to absorb assistance coincided with the appearance of the Chinese doctrine of wars of national liberation. At that time, it was recognized that this doctrine of self-help and absorptive capacity would not be adequate to cope with challenges to the security of Southeast Asia. There was also, therefore, a security-related category of foreign aid designed to assist such countries as South Vietnam, Laos, and Thailand to carry the burden of military preparations and operations. Out of this situation, two other doctrines for foreign assistance emerged. These doctrines were called political development and counter-insurgency.

Political development is an ambiguous idea. At the very least, it can mean one of two things: either the emergence or strengthening of democratic political life, or the development of a greater capacity to maange the state's public affairs. These two things are not necessarily the same.

In the body of thought guiding foreign assistance, political development is something that foreign assistance itself can affect. Thus, in security situations in Southeast Asia, thinking moved from discrimination in terms of self-help and absorptive capacity to the notion of using foreign aid to develop political capability in the recipient government.

The character of the problem has been most clear in the cases of Laos and South Vietnam. In Thailand, U.S. assistance is also justified mainly on grounds of security. This kind of justification was appropriate, because, on the one hand, although Thailand's economic strength is relatively great, on the other hand, the Kingdom is threatened by hostile external powers brandishing the weapons of revolutionary war. For these reasons, political development in Thailand is interpreted as the growing capacity to maintain *both* internal security and economic growth.

The doctrine of counterinsurgency might be considered a special case of political development. Rural insurrection is deemed an outcome of defective government in an unmobilized agricultural society that has been disrupted by one or more forces, such as organized, foreign-supported revolutionaries, commercial activities, "modernization," as well as war and invasion. Counterinsurgency is a response to a situation of rural insurrection by a combination of military efforts that combat the armed elements of insurrection and political efforts that reconstruct relations between the government and people. The reconstruction is designed to increase control of the population and to increase their satisfactions, loyalty, and structured commitment to the existing regime. Foreign assistance, in resources and technology, is thought to have a contribution to make to these various efforts.

How does foreign assistance look from the Thai point of view? It is not without its difficulties. Foreign assistance, either military or economic, is provided within a framework of obligations. Most assistance is linked to specifically agreed upon projects. These projects are mutually designed and planned by either the military assistance group or the AID mission on the U.S. side and, on the Thai side, a service or agency of the government. These agreements stipulate what is to be accomplished, when and how it is to be accomplished, and who is to contribute what resources and services to the project. Thus, foreign assistance is not a bundle of free resources that constitute merely an addition to local resources. Rather, it is a set of commitments to undertake certain kinds of activities.

The U.S. contribution, generally, is in terms of those things —resources or services—that can be paid for in U.S. dollars. The Thai Government is obliged to carry the project costs, which can be paid for in local currency. Thus, in the period 1951–65, when U.S. grants to assistance projects totalled $290 million, the Thai counterpart cost was the equivalent of about $70 million. So, in each case, the Thai Government must estimate the effect of the project on its own budget. The effect varies a great deal, but, because, in most cases, the government must take over the operation of the project after it is initiated, the character of the financial commitment is not fully reflected in the relative size of the initial contribution.

In addition to a financial commitment, these projects involve a commitment of people. People with skills are scarce in Thailand, as they are the world over, so that a commitment to assigning people to implement one kind of program in comparison with another is similar to a commitment of material resources. The U.S. assistance contribution to a project commonly includes a training component on the assumption that people are scarce, but the larger commitment of high-level managers for projects is a more difficult matter than mere training.

Therefore, even if foreign assistance is thought of as mainly a matter of implementing projects, the Thai Government is faced with difficult decisions of money and personnel. The difficulty is not merely a matter of scarce resources, however. Such decisions also have implications for the configuration of political power within the country. The leadership of the government must also ponder these political implications when they are deciding whether or not to undertake a particular project. We will consider some of these political effects of foreign assistance after looking at the explicit objectives and means of the assistance programs at present.

Objectives and Programs

The assistance of the United States, coming through the separate channels of MAP and AID, falls into several categories which can most easily be understood by the objectives they seek to attain. These objectives are (1) defense against invasion, (2) internal security, and (3) economic growth.

Military Assistance

MAP has sought, since 1951, to improve the ability of Thai services to undertake conventional defense missions. Since

1955, within the framework of SEATO planning, the effort has been infused with some strategic conceptions to which notions of roles and missions have been attached. This military assistance program includes organization of force units, equipment of units, operational and staff training, and improvement of logistical facilities. The program is administered by personnel of the U.S. services attached to the Joint U.S. Military Assistance Group, which is commanded by an American general. Since 1965, the Military Assistance Command–Thailand has been superimposed upon the JUSMAG organization-structure. Both groups have approximately the same personnel. These two agencies operate under the U.S. Commander in Chief, Pacific, and, through him, are responsible to the Joint Chiefs of Staff and the Assistant Secretary of Defense for International Security Affairs.

The second major mission of U.S. military forces in Thailand is internal security. This mission has always been a component of U.S. military assistance, but its importance rose, in the 1960's, in the face of increasing alarm about revolutionary warfare in Vietnam and insurrection, however minor, in Thailand.

The role of the Thai military forces in internal security is not a simple one, and the appropriate interpretation of the mission has proven to be difficult. Because military organization has served as a base of political power for many years, the role of internal security overlaps substantially with the political role. For example, the deployment of troops is determined in large part by the political requirement to have a sizable number of loyal troops in and around Bangkok. The First Army Command, the First Division, and other forces, are permanently stationed in the capital. These troops are available for only limited operations outside the Bangkok area. This characteristic of Thailand's military deployment has been a source of consternation and confusion to the U.S. military assistance effort.

The reasons for the confusion are to be found in conflicts over priorities between JUSMAG and the Thai military command. The differences have never been public ones, and it is difficult to know whether or not they have ever been made explicit by the agencies concerned. Nevertheless, it is very likely that the lack of agreement on some difficult matters— such as the likelihood of various, possibly threatening, contingencies and the appropriate deployment of units, assignment of missions, and, perhaps, even the equipment and training entailed by analysis of these contingencies—has diminished the effectiveness of U.S. assistance.

The conflict between JUSMAG and the Thai, as it relates to internal security, has been partially solved in recent years by defining the internal security mission more explicitly as one of counterinsurgency. This definition is justified by the appropriate assumption that insurgents, generally meaning *rural* insurgents, are the proxy forces of foreign powers, meaning Hanoi and Peking. Within MAP, there is agreement, then, that counterinsurgency is a top priority and is, therefore, supported by training, organization operations, and equipment deemed by Thai and U.S. military experts to be appropriate to the suppression of rural insurgents.

This limited agreement, however, has not answered the questions that have plagued the U.S. program for years: Has military assistance enhanced the combat effectiveness of Thai forces commensurate with the cost, and should military assistance be expected to accomplish that "narrow" end? The U.S. Secretaries of Defense, particularly Robert S. McNamara, have properly been concerned that military assistance accomplish something beneficial, such as, for example, an enhanced combat effectiveness. There is considerable evidence that military assistance to Thailand has seriously fallen short of normal U.S. expectations in this kind of effectiveness. The difficulty can best be attributed to the failure to agree on the general role of the military in Thailand, and, particularly, the very substantial political element of that role. Because of political reasons (which often affect the organization, deployment, officer assignment, and allocation of resources to different services and units), the military command in Thailand has been reluctant and, often, unwilling to make changes that might seem appropriate from a purely combat point of view. In practice, the military assistance program has usually accepted the outcome of such considerations without explicitly accepting the political reasons. This practice has confused, if not invalidated, the evaluations of the military assistance program.

The question of whether military assistance ought to be evaluated on criteria of combat effectiveness arises out of this situation. It is argued that, in order to attain the diplomatic influence the United States seeks in Thailand, it is necessary to accept, at least tacitly, the political role of the Thai military and accommodate U.S. expectations to it. Therefore, attempts to measure elements of the program in combat terms will lead to confusion. A counterargument holds that, because certain parts of the Thai military have combat roles in counterinsurgency and defense, U.S. assistance should be selectively addressed to them. If this were the practice, normal measures of effectiveness would be valid. This dispute remains unresolved.

Police

The internal security objective is shared by the military and the police. Therefore, U.S. assistance to police from AID sources is also aimed toward this objective. Outside of Bangkok, the Thai countryside is policed by the Provincial Police Division of the National Police Department, which has command over the regular Provincial Police, based in each provincial and district seat, and the Border Patrol Police, responsible for districts on the borders and, particularly, remote areas with minority populations.

The mission of the Provincial Police is complex, and the force not entirely adequate to it. It has the duty of policing the towns of the provincial areas, patrolling the rural areas to maintain law and order, and, recently, suppressing insurgents in those areas where they are operating. The weakness of the police is that they tend to be deployed mainly in the cities and towns. Their rural operations have been minimal and routine. Provincial Police have not been above petty extortion and, at the same time, are often ineffective in the apprehension of bandits and cattle thieves. The number of policemen, their age, and the equipment and facilities available to them have not been adequate for the job of active rural patrolling, so that low morale and lack of discipline in the rural police are common.

In recent years, the United States assistance program has invested substantially in better police work, mainly in the areas of training and equipping the rural police. As part of the police project, the United States has persuaded the government to increase the number of police stations and policemen in rural areas.

Whether or not the Provincial Police can be transformed from its present condition into an effective force for honest law enforcement and genuine protection of the lives and property of rural householders constitutes a critical test of the Thai Government's capacity to cope with its problems. Not only insurrection, but also the widespread increase in activity in rural Thailand, requires better police work.

Rural Development

According to the doctrines of counterinsurgency and political development, greater attention to the needs of the rural population is required to meet the challenge of potential insurrection. In order to move toward this end, the Thai Government and the U.S. assistance program have started a comprehensive operation called Accelerated Rural Development

(ARD). This operation is intended to make provincial governments better able to carry on development work in rural areas.

ARD is part of a general problem of local government in rural areas. The villages of Thailand have considerable autonomy but few resources. As long as their problems remained local and minor, this *laissez faire* system was adequate. However, in the face of external intervention, either in the form of attempts to mobilize people for political action or merely in the form of economic forces in the market, a more effective system of assessing the situation and distributing available resources is required. Changes of this sort have brought out a three-way tension among the ideas of traditional centralized administration, local self-government, and revolutionary mobilization. The problem is complicated by the failure of agreement between local communities and units of the central government. At present, the problems involved in this confusion have not been worked out. Although there have been many and various attempts to get some local government started, the results have been negligible. So the programs of local development are implemented by the central administration and are able to draw very little energy and few resources from the public.

The ARD program established a provincial construction facility for building roads and other necessary things such as small reservoirs. This facility is supposed to be the nucleus of a local government with the ability to plan and implement works and programs in response to the local situation. The Thai Government provides the staff and assumes responsibility for continuing operations, while U.S. assistance provides equipment and training. Since 1965, the ARD has been set up in provinces in northeastern and northern Thailand more or less according to calculations of security requirements.*

The efforts in rural development, while moved by security

* There is one ARD province in south central Thailand that is supported by the Thai Government without U.S. assistance.

objectives, contribute to economic growth. As one official said, "Economic development is the constructive by-product of this war." Efforts to improve the marketing of agricultural products and to increase production by organization of credit and technical assistance play an important part in the rural development program. For years, many of the attempts to affect agriculture have been unsullied by economic considerations. Many of them have failed for that reason. As the years of failure have accumulated, with their few unforeseen successes, such as the upsurge of feed corn production in response to market opportunities, more sophistication and competence have crept into the thinking behind these efforts. Nevertheless, it appears that the government's resources and staff, despite U.S. assistance, will not be sufficient to stimulate and manage the vast and complex task of transforming agriculture. Without the ambitions and efforts of private business, the task would be hopeless. But, as we saw before, private business is active, and changes are in the making. The government's task is to control and support this activity rather than to compete with it.

The government has triumphed, however, in the construction of dams, canals, roads, telephone systems, and port facilities. These require capital so large that only the government can accumulate it. Foreign assistance both from the United States and other countries and institutions is the principal source of the capital. The government has managed its foreign borrowing effectively, and political competence helps the country's credit rating.

Political competence of this sort depends upon administration and education. Political decisions require organizations to implement them, to find the resources for them, to assign them to various enterprises, and to see that they are used as intended. These organizations need educated and disciplined people. U.S. foreign assistance has contributed to these processes of administration and education.

This brief review of the range of government activities and

programs affected by foreign assistance brings us to several conclusions. First of all, as a recipient of foreign assistance, the government of Thailand has attained a sophistication that leads to fairly coherent objectives for the country as a whole and a use of foreign aid that is consistent with these coherent objectives. The degree of this consistency depends, to some extent, on the agencies providing assistance; they also influence coherence of objectives. But, in the end, this coherence is the outcome of political decisions imposed on the process of receiving aid, political decisions that both Thailand and the source of aid share.

A second appropriate conclusion seems to be that the programs related to foreign assistance are fairly effective. The problem of assessment, again, is not easy, because the objectives of defense, internal security, and economic growth imply many imponderables both in the present and future. At present, the measures of these objectives (e.g., no invasion, little insurgency, and rising per capita income) that we have give encouraging indications, but none of these objectives is finally attained. Each is a moving, shifting, dynamic set of problems that demands continuing action.

Unforeseen Consequences

It is the unforeseen, unintended, or ulterior consequences of such actions that we must now consider. Does foreign assistance lead to consequences for either the United States or Thailand that are so bad that they overshadow the benefits?

It is alleged that military assistance from the United States has led to military dictatorship in Thailand or, at least, maintains it. Leaving aside the question of whether or not the Thai system of government can be properly described as a military dictatorship, to what extent does U.S. military assistance influence the military character of the government? It is a fact that, since 1933, with the exception of a few years,

Thailand has had a government politically dominated by soldiers, whereas U.S. military assistance commenced no earlier than 1950. It is unlikely that the support of the United States in 1950 was anticipated by foresighted Thai soldiers in 1933. In short, there is no way in which it can be argued that U.S. assistance brought about military-dominated government.

Nevertheless, the influence of the U.S. assistance program on maintaining military dominance, as well as on the character of the military organization, is a question of interest. If we look at the Defense Ministry budget for the period 1959–65, we can see an indication of the influence of the military, in contrast to the influence of soldiers, in the country. We find that the budget for the military has varied from ฿ 1,433,-202,778,* in 1959, down to ฿ 1,110,095,864, in 1961, and then has risen to ฿ 1,920,600,000, in 1965. As a percentage of the national budget it has fallen from more than 18 per cent to about 15.5 per cent. The value of military assistance has annually been about $40 million in U.S. currency or about ฿ 800 million. This amount represents a significant portion (nearly half) of the military expenditures in Thailand and a relaxation of military pressure on the Thai budget. In sum, during this period covering the military governments of Field Marshals Sarit and Thanom, the part of national revenues spent on military affairs decreased at least partly because the United States paid the difference.

This situation could be interpreted in several ways. Supporting the idea that U.S. assistance maintains military government and, therefore, should be stopped, one could argue that forcing the Thai military budget completely onto the Thai people would result in an intolerable burden, against which they would revolt, overthrowing their military-dominated government and substituting for it a representative regime. This new regime would presumably reduce the military burden. A second and more likely interpretation is that U.S.

* 20.6 *bahts* (฿) = $1.00.

assistance has helped the soldier-dominated government to control the military demands on it, and, if the assistance were withdrawn, the burden would be shifted into the regular Thai budget, and the military services would be to that extent more involved and influential on government policy. The increment of ฿ 800 million would be about 6 per cent of the budget. Whether or not the shifting of 6 per cent within the budget, or even an increase of 6 per cent in expenditures, would result in a revolutionary change in the structure of Thai politics cannot be absolutely predicted, but it seems doubtful.

Another kind of influence of the military aid program, one that is much more difficult to assess, is its effect on the outlook of military officers. The way officers view their appropriate role in the community affects the way they act. The main thrust of U.S. training of Thai officers is certainly toward a more professional outlook that places high value on technical proficiency. There has always been something of a schism among Thai officers over whether to place a higher value on military or political technique. A view that the military should withdraw from politics in order better to prepare for its combat role has had its adherents. American programs of training for officers have supported this view and contributed to the growth of a group of young, competence-oriented officers. It is unlikely, however, that such a group would, on its own initiative, be able to end soldier-dominated government. Accomplishing that end would require not only willingness on the part of military officers to subordinate themselves to civilian control but also an organizational substitute for the power generated by military organization, a substitute somehow available to civilian politicians. At present, no such substitute exists.

Yet, U.S. assistance is not without influence in Thai politics, both among factions and in terms of policy. Assistance is usually allocated on the prospect of accomplishing a certain job. It is allocated as assistance to certain agencies that are supposed to be able to do the job. Usually, this supposition is based on formal responsibility, and assistance is designed to improve existing performance. Thus, assistance aimed at maintaining law and order is designed to improve police performance. Sometimes assistance is allocated to an agency on the basis of past performance. For example, in order to speed construction of rural roads, assistance went toward creating a new rural development operation (ARD) within the relatively effective Local Administration Department, rather than to the Highway Department, whose past performance was judged less effective.

These decisions on allocations often contribute substantially to the range of activities of a particular department or agency and enhance the positions of its leaders. An assessment of the effect of this influence is very difficult. It tends marginally to strengthen the influence of the already strong and to do little for the weak.

As is somewhat the case in military assistance, however, economic assistance tends to strengthen the political position of those who approach their work rationally and with technical competence. U.S. assistance, together with assistance from other industrial countries, the World Bank, the Asian Development Bank, and the United Nations, stands behind a loose faction of Western trained, rationalist, and technically competent officials in many departments and services. This faction, however, is not a cohesive political power, but, rather, represents a coherent attitude toward government. In this way, foreign assistance tends to encourage a greater margin of rationality in any decision.

This influence is only marginal, not dominant. Foreign assistance is only a small fraction of the resources at the disposal of the Thai Government, but this fraction, managed by competent people, has an influence greater than its size. Since it is, for the most part, devoted to change and novelty, the influence in the direction of change is that much enhanced. In the end, however, the leverage of foreign assistance alone is not sufficient to produce major modifications in the relationships of political and military factions, much less modifications in the constitutional structure of the government.

IX

The United States
and the Future of Thailand

American influence in Thailand is substantial but contingent. It derives from neither right and law, nor a long history of closeness. Rather, it flows out of the coincidence of interest, as demonstrated mainly in the actions and attitudes of the United States in Thailand, in Asia, and in the Pacific area—actions and attitudes designed to restrain the hostile influences of China and Vietnam and to support a world of open commerce and economic growth. In short, it is a purely political influence.

Foreign assistance has been, since 1950, a basic element of substance in the relationship between the two countries. Thailand has accepted the assistance of the United States in the realms of both security and development, accepted it on the terms offered and within the policy environment from which it flowed. The basically satisfactory nature of foreign assistance is closely related to two concepts of its political character. The first is that the policies of the United States have been consistent with the interests and aspirations of the government of Thailand. Secondly, the conditions of acceptance have not directly challenged the fundamentals of Thai political life.

Thus, the development of foreign assistance has followed after the political considerations of mutual interest. The willingness of the United States to maintain this relationship depends on continuing political convergence and an assessment that the incremental contributions to the economic, military, and administrative capacities of Thailand and its government will make it possible for the Thai Government to maintain its policies, which, in turn, contribute to the interests of the United States in Southeast Asia. In this way, America gains influence in Thailand.

But influence also emerges from a larger framework of action. The strategic position of the United States in the Pacific and Southeast Asia is a fundamental of American influence. The emplacement of commitments and forces throughout the region constitutes an immensely impressive position. The United States is bound by treaty to assist in the defense of South Korea, Japan, Taiwan, the Philippines, Thailand, Australia, and New Zealand. It has deployed forces—air, sea, and ground—to implement those commitments, if it should become necessary.

The intervention of massive force in both Korea and Vietnam has, of course, been the culmination of this structure of commitments from which the influence of the United States in Asia derives. Thailand has been deeply impressed by the willingness to fulfill the commitments, as demonstrated by the deployment of troops.

The Thai Government has also been impressed by the political reaction in the United States to this troop deployment. Because the political reaction has included a severe inquiry into the validity of policies and attitudes that stand behind the Vietnam involvement, it has become clear to the Thai that the power and influence of the United States must rest ultimately on the political will of the American Government. The strength of that will is ultimately contingent upon forces over which the Thai have no influence.

The Thai Government and, substantially, the Thai people do not share the view that Thailand is part of China's "natural sphere of influence." Without immediately delving into the ambiguities of the notion of spheres of influence, we can accept the fact that the consistent American position of opposition to the expansion of the Chinese influence into Thailand, among other places, has been the foundation of American influence in Thailand. Should the position change, the influence of the United States in Thailand would certainly change its basis and probably, of necessity, decline.

In addition to the anti-Chinese position of the United States, American opposition to the unification of Vietnam under a powerful (presumably North Vietnamese) government has contributed to United States influence. The perennial struggle between the Thai and Vietnamese for influence over the areas and peoples of present-day Laos and Cambodia remains unsettled to this day. The Thai Government views American intervention in Vietnam as the current salient of this struggle, as well as a part of the resistance to China.

The American Government conceives of its intervention in Vietnam, however, as a forward strategy in the defense of Japan, on the north, and Australia, on the south, as well as an intrinsic defense of Southeast Asia from Chinese control or influence. It is, therefore, possible to foresee contingencies in which the United States would accept a strategic withdrawal to another line of defense that does not include Thailand. The Thai Government is not unaware of that possibility and must make calculations with that in mind. Its recognition of the contingent character of the American strategic attitudes regarding Southeast Asia attenuates the influence that flows out of the commitments.

Nevertheless, the influence is very great and is strengthened by a more generalized and intangible aspect of the position of the United States in the world. This aspect might be called the attitudes informing American imperialism. This is an age of nationalisms, more or less responsibly managed in a great number of small states. It is often necessary for the United States, because of its great power, which ramifies politically, economically, and militarily throughout the world, to involve itself in the affairs of small states. Such involvement represents a continuing effort to find an order for world affairs within which peace and justice may be found. This effort to find an order—an effort not necessarily well conceived, free of failure, nor lacking in the use of force and power—is the substance of American imperialism.

The American effort has three notable characteristics. One is the assumption that autonomous states should conduct their own internal affairs constrained only by the requirement for peaceful relations with other states; in short, an assumption of a community of free nations. The second characteristic is a relatively open attitude toward economic and social organization. The third characteristic of the attitudes underlying American imperialism is the belief that change should come about peacefully. All of these characteristics are, of course, enshrined in the concepts of the United Nations.

Implementation of American imperialism is by no means free of difficulties and inconsistencies. Practical judgments on the freedom to join the camp of the enemy or to seize the property of Americans for whatever good cause have been made for the most part according to a standard of benefit to the United States. The exertion of alternative influences from such great and major powers as the Soviet Union or the People's Republic of China, based on a conception to some degree conflicting with the American vision, has led to antagonism and struggle. In Southeast Asia, particularly in Vietnam but, perhaps, potentially in Thailand as well, such struggle has centered on the issue of changes in the nation's internal political efforts.

The U.S. emphasis on both internal autonomy and peaceful change has led to an often obtuse American reaction to the problems of social transformation. In the course of internal change in unmobilized or mobilizing societies, the structure of political status and rights becomes an obstacle that cannot be overcome by established and peaceful means. Such a state of affairs frequently results in violent political action that is aimed toward some reordering of politics. America has no consistent and effective doctrine for this sort of situation.

In contrast, just such a doctrine is central to Communist thought and it informs the influence of the Soviet Union and China. Along this route marches the specter of expanding Communist influence hostile to the American vision of international order. This defect of American thought and actions—this lack of a doctrine of revolutionary change—has led to the costly enterprise in Vietnam.

Nevertheless, the American vision of world order based on autonomous nations—a vision characterized by liberality—is attractive to small states such as Thailand. American influence, because it is undemanding as well as powerful in most respects, is more welcome than the influence of others.

Why should the United States seek to maintain or extend its influence in Thailand and Southeast Asia? Some assessment of its cost in comparison to its benefits is justified, because such influence depends upon a continuing, costly effort to uphold a strategic position, to maintain an assistance program, and to sustain an imperial attitude. The lives lost in Vietnam are precious, and the billions of dollars expended there are not without value in terms of other things foregone. From slums, to schools, to space, there have been and will be opportunities for the use of the wealth and energy spent in Southeast Asia.

The war in Vietnam has been excessively costly. Therefore, it is right that we assess the risks of becoming a part of another unmanageable and unpredictable struggle in another place, for example, Thailand—a struggle that we do not initiate, do not understand, and, once caught in, cannot escape. In short, is Thailand likely to be "another Vietnam?"

On the basis of the preceding chapters, it is clear that Thailand and Vietnam are very different. Thailand has a long history of independence and effective self-government, a government that is coping with the problems of social and economic change. Unlike the Vietnamese, the Thai have only a slight tradition of insurrection. The inequalities of wealth and status in Thai society, however great, are justified, to a great extent, by a still vital tradition of religiously sanctioned subordination. With a few exceptions, Thailand is free of the brutalizing, direct exploitations of large, absentee landlords or uncontrolled bureaucrats.

Thailand is not free of defects or injustices, as the preceding chapters make clear. To say that there is no possibility of a collapse of authority or a widespread insurrection would be absurd. Nevertheless, the broad and genuine differences of all kinds between the political, economic, and social situations in Thailand and Vietnam make comparisons impossible. The assertion, frequently made, that revolutionary development in Thailand today is similar to that in Vietnam in 1945 or 1956 or 1959 or whenever is absurd and without foundation.

It is probably not possible that Thailand could be brought to the condition of Vietnam. The only way that it might move in that direction is that if both the United States and the Chinese, mutually agreeing that it is about to become so, were to invest heavily in their efforts to cope with that prophecy and, thereby, fulfill it. The marginal disruption of foreign-supported efforts toward revolution, sufficiently reinforced by counterinsurgent activities, could become significant.

Thus, the risk of disruption of the society of Thailand is not zero, but it does appear that the prudence required of both the government of Thailand and its ally, the United States, may be reasonably expected and that the risk is low enough to make it less than compelling as a reason to discontinue the commitments of the United States to Thailand.

Nevertheless, at the present moment of reconsideration of

U.S. policy in Southeast Asia and Thailand, a broader view of the issues is required than one based on whether Thailand may become another Vietnam. These issues can be grouped around the reasonable objectives that may induce the United States to continue its active relationship with Thailand. There are two sets of objectives that may be served through such a relationship. One set is related to policing the peace, if any, of Southeast Asia. The second set is contributing to the building of cohesion and cooperation in the area, from which may emerge a basis for regional power and stability. These objects are not incompatible with each other. Both sets of objects have their attendant risks as well as benefits.

Seeking to attain these objectives through a continuing relationship with Thailand makes sense when it is recognized that Thailand is the strongest national community in Southeast Asia. Its strength lies neither in its industrial capacity (although its agricultural production is not a negligible factor) nor in its military ability but, rather, in its political capacity— its historically demonstrated ability to cope with its problems and to generate power and authority on the basis of cohesion and cooperation. In that respect, it is substantially more impressive than most of its neighbors. When this capacity is coupled with the fact of a substantial and productive population, Thailand stands out as a place of strength in an unpredictable region.

The objective of policing a peace in Southeast Asia will take on an organized meaning only as the character of a Vietnam settlement becomes clear. If it is assumed that this settlement involves the establishment of a formally independent and autonomous South Vietnam, the critical consideration will be the arrangements for enforcing the terms. The basic element of this consideration will be the degree to which the United States will participate as a guarantor or enforcer.

The international agreements in regard to Vietnam, negotiated at Geneva in 1954, failed in substantial part, because the responsibility for enforcing them was highly diffuse. The Democratic Republic of Vietnam (North Vietnam) and France negotiated an armistice, and those two parties, plus a number of others, negotiated a complicated and, in some ways, ambiguous general agreement. This latter was to be "enforced" by the cochairmen, Britain and the Soviet Union, through the intrinsically powerless International Control Commission. Because none of these parties (with the exception of North Vietnam) was willing and able to do very much about it, the interpretation and implementation of the international agreements failed. From that failure followed the intervention of the United States and the emergence of South Vietnam as an independent state. Most international agreements are only as effective as the responsible parties care to make them, and the 1954 accord was no exception.

For this reason, the demonstration of the American assumption of responsibility in implementing Vietnam agreement will be a critical element in the significance of that agreement. It is very likely that the position of the United States in Thailand would be a part of this demonstration. The costs sunk in facilities, the long record of fruitful association, and the probable interest of the Thai Government in maintaining an independent South Vietnam combine to form both a reason and a basis for cooperation between the United States and Thailand in some form of peace-keeping.

What applies to Vietnam applies even more to Laos and Cambodia. The protection of their independence and integrity—whether or not South Vietnam remains independent—will require the cooperation of the United States and Thailand. Thus, if the notion of dominoes falling—Vietnam, then Laos and Cambodia, and so on—is not to come true, some effort to prevent it cannot be avoided.

The notion of falling dominoes is merely a metaphor. Nevertheless, if the United States abruptly terminates its cooperation with the states in Southeast Asia, particularly Thailand, some advancement of Vietnamese and Chinese influence is highly probable. A threat of rapidly expanding Communist influence cannot be simply dismissed on the grounds that the "domino theory" is no theory, or that the Chinese and Vietnamese have not yet expanded.

If such an expansion develops, the relationship of power in Asia will become pregnant with threats. The threat from China, with nuclear arms and allies on the Gulf of Siam, would constitute a new kind of threat to both Japan and India. In such an eventuality, both of these states might well feel compelled to produce their own nuclear weapons as a deterrent. The specter of proliferation of nuclear weapons throughout Asia, and, perhaps, throughout the entire world, is a formidable prospect.

Policing the peace, however, while profoundly important, is a static and, perhaps, sterile notion. In the longer run, the United States must seek, and be willing to contribute to, the establishment of a self-maintaining order in Southeast Asia. The present outlines of such a future order are dim. Any discussion of the character or shape of a future Southeast Asia that is orderly and self-perpetuating would be highly speculative.

If an order of that kind is to come from the present, it will emerge from a clash of visions that are more or less contradictory. One such vision is presumably held by some Chinese leaders, a vision that involves a set of Communist regimes which submit themselves to the leadership of the Chinese Communist Party. An alternative is the view, apparently held by former President Sukarno, of Indonesia, of a grouping of radically progressive regimes, "new, emerging forces," under the hegemony of a dynamic Indonesia, the largest state of the area. Another conception of a future Southeast Asia, adhered to, in various inchoate forms, by several statesmen of Southeast Asia, is a regionalism of equality among a number of states, from which wealth and power can spring. It is possible to imagine that the United States may offer a vision of the area in which America seeks to acquire and maintain a hegemony over these weak states.

Evidence of previous American experience, however, indicates that such a notion would be imprudent, not only because it is unfeasible, but also because, even in the short run, it might reduce American influence, which depends substantially on minimal interference. A more effective policy would be to reinforce, by declaration and substantial assistance of resources and technique, centers of cohesion that would serve as a basis for organizing power. Only by the maintenance and strengthening of such centers is it possible to expect the basis for effective forms of cooperation that may constitute an emergent regional order.

Thailand is such a center. Its capacity for self-rule is evidenced by an ability to make binding agreements as to both the use of resources and the implementation of cooperative policy. Its social solidarity and its potential for economic and political growth combine to make Thailand an appropriate point of access for U.S. influence.

The government of Thailand has already declared its adherence to a vision of regional cooperation in Southeast Asia. Its participation in the Association of Southeast Asia (ASA) and the Association of Southeast Asian Nations (ASEAN) has been earnest and as effective as can be expected. The contribution of Thailand to mitigation of the confrontation between Malaysia and Indonesia was sincere and useful. Other examples of Thailand's role in the search for future regional cooperation might be readily adduced.*

* In addition to ASA and ASEAN, Thailand has participated actively in the following regional groupings: Southeast Asia League, Economic Commission for Asia and the Far East (ECAFE), Mekong Development Committee, Southeast Asia Treaty Organization (SEATO), Asian and Pacific Council (ASPAC), Southeast Asian Ministers of Education Secretariat (SEAMES), Ministerial Conferences on Economic Development in Southeast Asia, and the Asian Development Bank (ADB).

If the United States is prepared to participate in this quest in a manner that neither threatens an oppressive American hegemony nor is merely a trivial and expedient gesture, its influence must go to the existing centers of order with the purpose of bringing about a basis and process for broader cooperation.

Thailand not only qualifies as a relatively cohesive and solid social community that has a record of effective use of assistance within a situation of domestic order, but it is also strategically placed in regard to the obstacles to and opportunities for expanding regional cooperation. It is an interested and active participant in the affairs of the Lower Mekong, not only in the conflicts and battles among the peoples of former French colonies, but also in the efforts to develop the potential of this great basin.*

Thailand has also been a participant in the various efforts of the Malay nations to find a basis for cooperation among themselves. These three nations, Malaysia, the Philippines, and Indonesia—with a combined population of, perhaps, 140 million people—are of profound importance in Southeast Asia. The basis for their cooperation has proved elusive, but it is significant that Thailand, a country of non-Malay people, has been active in the quest.

Another obstacle to order in Southeast Asia is the unsettled political condition of the various ethnic groups in the mountains ranging across Vietnam, Laos, Thailand, Burma, and southern China. These people—some Thai-speaking, some of other linguistic and ethnic backgrounds—are in various states of conflict with the dominant lowland folk. While Thailand has no unique success to its credit, it has access to this turbulent area.

A final salient difficulty of Southeast Asian nations is the status of their so-called overseas Chinese populations.

* The headquarters of the four-nation Mekong Development Committee has been located in Bangkok for fifteen years.

Throughout the area, people of Chinese background live as more or less self-conscious communities, whose continued search for a unique cultural identity as well as actual or potential connections with China cause them to be treated with suspicion. There is one small state—Singapore—that is overwhelmingly Chinese, while Malaysia has a minority of more than 40 per cent. All the other states have smaller, but important, minority Chinese groups. Thailand's rather successful policy of assimilation of its Chinese minority may be a fruitful model in other places.

Thailand falls well short of anyone's conception of a perfect community. With an unsettled constitution, an underdeveloped economy, and an unmobilized society, the leaders of the Thai nation face formidable obstacles and threats to the order and justice of their community. Nevertheless, they have a record of some success, and reason for confidence that success may continue. The future of Thailand seems to promise an opportunity for the United States to contribute to the realization of the sort of world it wishes.

By using the influence America has in accordance with guidelines appropriate to both its potentiality and its limits, the United States may return to its role as a wealthy and ingenious contributor to the construction of a better world order.

Further Reading

SOUTHEAST ASIA

History and Sociology

BASTIN, JOHN, and BENDA, HARRY J. *A History of Modern Southeast Asia.* Englewood Cliffs, N. J.: Prentice-Hall, 1968.

CADY, JOHN. *Southeast Asia: Its Historical Development.* New York: McGraw-Hill, 1964.

DuBOIS, CORA. *Social Forces in Southeast Asia.* Cambridge, Mass.: Harvard University Press, 1949.

HALL, D. G. E. *A History of South-East Asia.* London: St. Martin's Press, 1964.

HEINE-GELDERN, ROBERT. *Concepts of State and Kingship in Southeast Asia.* Ithaca, N. Y.: Cornell University Press, 1956.

KUNSTADTER, PETER, ed. *Southeast Asian Tribes, Minorities, and Nations.* Princeton, N. J.: Princeton University Press, 1967.

MYRDAL, GUNNAR. *Asian Drama: An Inquiry into the Poverty of Nations.* New York: The Twentieth Century Fund, 1968.

ONSLOW, CRANELY, ed. *Asian Economic Development.* New York: Praeger, 1965.

PURCELL, VICTOR. *The Chinese in Southeast Asia.* 2d ed. London: Oxford University Press, 1965.

WERTHEIM, WILLEM FREDERIK. *East-West Parallels.* The Hague: Van Hoeve, 1964.

WILLIAMS, LEA. *The Future of the Overseas Chinese in Southeast Asia.* New York: McGraw-Hill, 1966.

Politics and Regional Security

BARNETT, A. DOAK. *Communist Strategies in Asia.* New York: Praeger, 1963.

BRIMMEL, J. H. *Communism in Southeast Asia: A Political Analysis.* London: Oxford University Press, 1959.

CROZIER, BRIAN. *Southeast Asia in Turmoil.* Rev. ed. London: Penguin, 1968.

FIFIELD, RUSSELL F. *Southeast Asia in United States Policy.* New York: Praeger, 1963.

————. *The Diplomacy of Southeast Asia, 1945–1958.* New York: Harper, 1958.

GORDON, BERNARD K. "Southeast Asian View of China." *Current History* (September, 1968): 165–70.

————. *The Dimensions of Conflict in Southeast Asia.* Englewood Cliffs, N. J.: Prentice-Hall, 1966.

————. *Toward Disengagement in Asia.* Englewood Cliffs, N. J.: Prentice-Hall, 1969.

HANNA, WILLARD A. *Eight Nation-Makers: Southeast Asia's Charismatic Statesmen.* London: St. Martin's Press, 1964.

KAHIN, GEORGE McT., ed. *Governments and Politics of Southeast Asia.* 2d ed. Ithaca, N. Y.: Cornell University Press, 1964.

KENNEDY, D. K. *The Security of Southern Asia.* London: Institute for Strategic Studies, 1965.

MODELSKI, GEORGE. *SEATO: Six Studies.* Melbourne: F. W. Cheshire, Pty. Ltd., 1962.

MOZINGO, DAVID P. "Communist China: Its Southern Border Lands." *SAIS Review* 12 (Winter, 1968): 45.

————. "Containment in Asia Reconsidered." *World Politics* 19 (April, 1967): 361–77.

NIXON, RICHARD M. "Asia After Vietnam." *Foreign Affairs* 46 (October, 1967): 111–25.

PYE, LUCIAN, W. *Southeast Asia's Political Systems.* Englewood Cliffs, N. J.: Prentice-Hall, 1967.

REISCHAUER, EDWIN O. *Beyond Vietnam: The United States and Asia.* New York: Knopf, 1967.

SCALAPINO, ROBERT, ed. *The Communist Revolution in Asia.* Berkeley & Los Angeles: University of California Press, 1965.

TRAGER, FRANK, ed. *Marxism in Southeast Asia.* Stanford, Calif.: Stanford University Press, 1959.

YAHUDA, MICHAEL. "Chinese Foreign Policy After 1963: The Maoist Phases." *China Quarterly* (October–December, 1968): 93–113.

Laos, Cambodia, and Vietnam

CHAMPASSAK, SISOUK NA. *Storm over Laos.* New York: Praeger, 1961.

DOMMEN, ARTHUR J. *Conflict in Laos: The Politics of Neutralization.* New York: Praeger, 1964.

FALL, BERNARD B. *The Two Viet-Nams: A Political and Military Analysis.* Rev. ed. New York: Praeger, 1966.

————. *Viet-Nam Witness: 1953–66.* New York: Praeger, 1966.

GURTOV, MELVIN. *The First Vietnam Crisis.* New York: Columbia University Press, 1967.

HERZ, MARTIN F. *A Short History of Cambodia*. New York: Praeger, 1958.

LACOUTURE, JEAN. *Vietnam: Between Two Truces*. New York: Random House, Vintage, 1966.

PIKE, DOUGLAS. *Viet Cong: The Organization and Techniques of the National Liberation Front of South Vietnam*. Cambridge, Mass.: MIT Press, 1966.

SMITH, ROGER M. *Cambodia's Foreign Policy*. Ithaca, N. Y.: Cornell University Press, 1965.

TOYE, HUGH. *Laos: Buffer State or Battleground*. London: Oxford University Press, 1968.

THAILAND

General Reference and History

HARRIS, GEORGE L., ed., *et al*. *Area Handbook for Thailand* (Department of the Army Pamphlet No. 550–553). Washington, D. C.: American University Foreign Area Studies Division, Government Printing Office, 1966.

INSOR, D. *Thailand: A Political, Social, and Economic Analysis*. New York: Praeger, 1963.

LANDON, KENNETH P. *Siam in Transition*. Chicago: University of Chicago Press, 1939.

Thailand Official Yearbook 1964. Bangkok: Government Printing Office.

VELLA, WALTER F. *The Impact of the West on Government in Thailand*. Berkeley & Los Angeles: University of California Press, 1955.

Ethnography and Anthropology

EMBREE, JOHN F. "Thailand: A Loosely-Structured Social System." *American Anthropologist* 52 (April-June, 1950): 181–93.

EVERS, H. D. "The Formation of a Social Class Structure: Urbanization, Bureaucratization and Social Mobility in Thailand." *Journal of Southeast Asian History* 7 (September, 1966): 100–105.

FRASER, THOMAS M., JR. *Fishermen of South Thailand: The Malay Villagers*. New York: Holt, Rinehart, & Winston, 1966.

HANKS, L. M. "Merit and Power in the Thai Social Order." *American Anthropologist* 64 (December, 1962): 1247–61.

MOERMAN, MICHAEL. "Western Culture and the Thai Way of Life." *Asia* (Spring, 1964): 31–50.

PHILLIPS, HERBERT P. *Thai Peasant Personality*. Berkeley & Los Angeles: University of California Press, 1965.

PIKER, STEVEN. "Sources of Stability and Instability in Rural Thai Society." *Journal of Asian Studies* 27 (August, 1968): 777–90.

————. "The Relationship of Belief Systems to Behavior in Rural Thai Society." *Asian Survey* 8 (May, 1968): 384–400.

YOUNG, GORDON. *The Hill Tribes of Northern Thailand.* Bangkok: The Siam Society, 1966.

Economic Development

AYAL, ELIEZER B. "Private Enterprise and Economic Progress in Thailand." *Journal of Asian Studies* 26 (November, 1966): 5–14.

FREEMAN, HAROLD. "Education as an Instrument of National Policy in Selected Newly Developing Nations. Phase 5, The Role of Agricultural Education in the Economic Development of Thailand" (Cooperative Research Project #1032). Stanford, Calif.: Comparative Education Center, School of Education, Stanford University, 1964.

HARING, JOSEPH E., and WESTPHAL, LARRY E. "Financial Policy in Postwar Thailand: External Equilibrium and Domestic Development." *Asian Survey* 8 (May, 1968): 364–78.

INGRAM, JAMES. *Economic Change in Thailand Since 1850.* Stanford, Calif.: Stanford University Press, 1955.

MOERMAN, MICHAEL. *Agricultural Choice and Peasant Choice in a Thai Village.* Berkeley & Los Angeles: University of California Press, 1968.

MUSCAT, ROBERT J. *Development Strategy in Thailand: A Study of Economic Growth.* New York: Praeger, 1966.

SILCOCK, T. H., ed. *Thailand: Social and Economic Studies in Development.* Durham, N. C.: Duke University Press, 1967.

YANU, TOTO. "Land Tenure in Thailand." *Asian Survey* 8 (October, 1968): 853–64.

Politics and National Integration

ISHII, YONEO. "Church and State in Thailand." *Asian Survey* 8 (October, 1968): 864–71.

KEYES, CHARLES FENTON. *Isan: Regionalism in Northeast Thailand* (Cornell Thailand Project, Interim Reports Series, 10). Ithaca, N. Y.: Cornell University Press, 1967.

PLATENIUS, HANS. *The Northeast of Thailand: Its Problems and Potentialities.* Bangkok: National Economic Development Board, 1963.

POOLE, PETER A. "Thailand's Vietnamese Refugees: Can They Be Assimilated?" *Pacific Affairs* 40 (Fall–Winter, 1967–68): 324–32.

RIGGS, FRED W. *Thailand: The Modernization of a Bureaucratic Polity.* Honolulu: East-West Center Press, 1966.

SIFFIN, WILLIAM J. *The Thai Bureaucracy: Institutional Change and Development.* Honolulu: East-West Center Press, 1966.

SKINNER, G. WILLIAM. *Chinese Society in Thailand: An Analytical History.* Ithaca, N. Y.: Cornell University Press, 1957.

———. *Leadership and Power in the Chinese Community of Thailand*. Ithaca, N. Y.: Cornell University Press, 1959.

———. "The Thai Chinese: Assimilation in a Changing Society." *Asia* (Autumn, 1964): 80–92.

STANDISH, W. A. "Malay Moslem Mixtures." *Far Eastern Economic Review* 57 (July 6, 1967): 18–22.

SUTTON, JOSEPH L., ed. *Problems of Politics and Administration in Thailand*. Bloomington, Indiana: Indiana University Press, 1962.

WILSON, DAVID A. *Politics in Thailand*. Ithaca, N. Y.: Cornell University Press, 1962.

———. "The Military in Thai Politics," in J. J. Johnson, ed., *The Role of the Military in Underdeveloped Countries*. Princeton, N. J.: Princeton University Press, 1962.

——— et al. "Symposium on the Northeast." *Asian Survey* 6 (July, 1966).

WIT, DANIEL. *Thailand: Another Vietnam?* New York: Scribner's, 1968.

YANO, TORU. "Sarit and Thailand's Pro-American Policy." *The Developing Economies* 6 (September, 1968): 284–99.

YOUNG, STEPHEN B. "The Northeastern Thai Village: A Non-Participatory Democracy." *Asian Survey* 8 (November, 1968): 873–86.

Foreign Relations

DARLING, FRANK C. *Thailand and the United States*. Washington, D. C.: Public Affairs Press, 1965.

HANKS, L. M. "American Aid is Damaging Thai Society." *Trans-action* 5 (October, 1968): 29–34.

KHOMAN, THANAT. "Which Road for Southeast Asia?" *Foreign Affairs* 42 (July, 1964): 628–39.

MODELSKI, GEORGE. "Thailand and China: From Avoidance to Hostility," in A. M. Halpern, ed., *Policies Toward China: Views from Six Continents*. New York: McGraw-Hill, 1965.

NUECHTERLEIN, DONALD E. "Thailand and SEATO: A Ten Year Appraisal." *Asian Survey* 4 (December, 1964): 1174–81.

WILSON, DAVID A. "China, Thailand, and the Spirit of Bandung." *China Quarterly* (April–June, 1967): 149–69, (July–September, 1967): 96–127.

Index